CHALLENGE
AND
RESPONSE

CHALLENGE AND RESPONSE

A HANDBOOK
OF CHRISTIAN APOLOGETICS

Frederic R. Howe

ZONDERVAN
PUBLISHING HOUSE
OF THE ZONDERVAN CORPORATION
GRAND RAPIDS, MICHIGAN 49506

CHALLENGE AND RESPONSE: A HANDBOOK OF CHRISTIAN APOLOGETICS
Copyright © 1982 by The Zondervan Corporation
Grand Rapids, Michigan

First printing, August 1982

Library of Congress Cataloging in Publication Data
Howe, Frederic R.
    Challenge and response, a handbook of Christian apologetics.
    Bibliography: p.
    1. Apologetics—20th century. I. Title.
BT1102.H69   239   82-2852
ISBN 0-310-45070-5   AACR2

Unless otherwise indicated, all Scripture quotations are from the *New American Standard Bible* © The Lockman Foundation 1960, 1962, 1963, 1968, 1971, 1972, 1973, 1975.

Edited by John Danilson and Gerard Terpstra
Designed by Louise Bauer

Printed in the United States of America

to my wife
Juanita

Contents

Foreword

I am not a specialist in the field of apologetics; so I read this manuscript from the same perspective that many of the readers of this book will have. And I can say with confidence that it provides one of the most helpful introductions to the subject of apologetics that I know about.

It is, as the title indicates, a handbook of Christian apologetics. One of its greatest strengths is that it is not simply a compilation of evidences for the truth of Christianity but a careful discussion of the issues involved in validating its claims. It orients the reader to the major questions in the field and explains the issues clearly and competently.

Another important strength of this work is the good theological and exegetical base on which it is erected. This keeps it on track and guards it from taking the wrong directions pursued by some writers. But this is as one would expect from the pen of a trained and experienced theologian.

Apologetics has been a lifelong interest of Dr. Howe. He has studied with leading apologists of the past and present generations and has himself taught in the field over many years. His erudition never gets in the way of clear communication.

The book charts a clear course through a field that is too often made obscure by its friends. Its relevance is unquestioned in this day when challenges to Christianity are on the increase and more blatantly so. This book will not only educate and strengthen the faith of the readers but it will also provide them with proper tools with which to defend their faith.

Charles C. Ryrie

Preface

This book is written as a guide to some of the areas within the broad field of Christian apologetics. It is hoped that it can serve as a tool for teachers, students, and others who are seeking information at the introductory level. Some very definite principles must be kept in focus as the book is used.

First, it is not intended as a development of any one particular system of apologetics. Rather, it should serve as a guide to an understanding of what apologetics is, where it fits into the framework of theological studies, and what can be expected as far as workable results from the data of this realm of information are concerned.

Second, it is not intended as a complete treatment of all the issues in apologetics. The term *handbook* in the title reflects selectivity in treatment of some crucial areas.

Third, a definite format has been followed. After establishing the major guidelines for studying apologetics, the approach, as suggested in the title, will be to state some challenges brought against Christianity and to offer specific responses to these challenges. They are:

—the challenge that comes concerning the existence of God and theistic argumentation in general. This area deals specifically with the *God of creation* and is an attempt to respond to the determined rejection of truth captured in the statement that "there is *no God*, no evidence to investigate concerning His existence."

—the challenge that comes concerning the revelation of God in history. Building on the first subject, this challenge deals specifically with God's authentic *communication* and is an attempt to respond to the implications of the negation that "there is *no certainty* for the historical claims for Christianity."

—the challenge that comes concerning the uniqueness of Christ and selected issues in the vindication of His supernatural origin and triumph over death in His resurrection. Continuing the theme of the second subject or challenge, this covers specifically God's ultimate *confrontation* with man in the person of the God-man, the Lord Jesus Christ. It is an attempt to discuss the ramifications of the negation that "there is *no uniqueness to Jesus* and His claims."

To be sure, there are many more issues in apologetics. The choice of these three is made with the full realization that one could feasibly deal with a defense of biblical orthodoxy at every segment of systematic theology. These three basic areas can form a meaningful ground for introducing the reader to this entire realm. The challenges raised in these three areas alone are so basic that they must be considered normative for a handbook on Christian defense.

I have attempted to define and defend a serious and sustained differentiation between the fields of apologetics and evangelism. I believe that with this differentiation firmly established in our thinking, a real and concerted effort to give a reason for our faith can go forward in complete reliance on the strength of Christ.

Furthermore, I have attempted to rest the work of defense on solid biblical groundwork. Realizing that Scripture must be central in the work of our institutions of Christian higher learning, I have attempted to offer biblical support for the principles enunciated. Also, I have attempted to deal with selected central passages of the Bible related to the confrontation between the Christian position and its challengers. I am keenly aware of the fact that we must do more than provide lip service to the dictum that Scripture and the biblical framework are basic for our education. I trust that the work will be useful in bringing glory to God and helping workers in the field of theological endeavors to contend earnestly for the faith.

CHAPTER 1

A Biblical Basis
For Apologetics

INTRODUCTION

The person who is beginning research and study in Christian apologetics is usually armed with some preconceptions with reference to this highly fascinating field of study. "The best defense is a good offense," we are told, and possibly the implication is that to make a systematic defense of the Christian faith is essentially to waste valuable time. It has been said that "apologetics usually consists of proving what you have never doubted by arguments that you don't understand."[1] This line of reasoning reveals an attitude of basic mistrust of any attempt to investigate the defense of the Christian faith. All talk of defensive strategy and detailed argumentation seems somehow strangely removed from the proclamation of the gospel of Christ and His triumph in individual lives. Christianity rests on great biblical truths. These truths include the vital orders of the Lord Jesus Christ, orders that are associated with advancement and achievement, not with negativism and defeat! Perhaps, therefore, Christian defensive or apologetic activity has been thought by some to involve compromise or, at best, stating the Christian view in such a manner that it will be acceptable to the mind of the unbeliever, thereby sacrificing the essentials of the faith. This being the case, we will begin our study by examining the nature of apologetics.

BIBLICAL TERMS RELATED TO APOLOGETICS

The word *apologetics* has a specific relationship to the Greek words *apologia* and *apologeomai*. Present-day usage of the adjective *apologetic* might explain why this whole realm of studies is sometimes viewed with distrust. When someone's tone or demeanor is "apologetic," the implication is clearly given that there is an acknowledgment of some kind of fault. Such a tone implies an attitude of concession or willingness to admit wrong and to "apologize" for the activity in question. However, this implication is really not in the picture at all when it comes to apologetics. In New Testament times the Greek noun *apologia* meant a statement or speech of defense or reply.[2] From the list of usages of this noun *apologia* in the New Testament, we can profitably select and examine several to see their bearing on our investigation. Acts 22:1 states, "Brethren and fathers, hear my defense [Greek, *apologia*] which I now *offer* to you." The elements involved in this activity of defense are all seen in this vivid example. Accusation had been leveled against the apostle Paul, and a careful answer, defense, or apology needed to be made. Paul proceeds to outline the personal factors in his life that would account for his presence in Jerusalem at that particular time. The answer given by Paul in this case, as in all of his speeches in defense, manifested an attitude of dignity and yet a forthright response to the issues. There was no condescension or dealing with his hearers in a patronizing manner. He spoke out clearly in an *apology* in this biblical sense.

Having gone to Rome as a prisoner because of the preaching of the gospel, Paul used his pen to encourage the churches. He wrote to the Philippians that "both in my imprisonment and in the defense [Greek, *apologia*] and confirmation of the gospel, you all are partakers of grace with me . . . knowing that I am appointed for the defense [*apologia*] of the gospel" (Phil. 1:7, 16). The clear Pauline implication here is that defense, as a statement of response to the charges or questions raised, is closely linked to the gospel. In fact, the major scope of the apostle Paul's ministry can easily be described with those very terms: defense and confirmation of the gospel. It appears that there is a definite pattern of usage and relationship suggested in Philippians 1 about this matter of the Christian message and the

Christian defense. Notice this progression:
—the furtherance of the gospel (v. 5)
—the defense and confirmation of the gospel (v. 7)
—the progress of the gospel (v. 12)
—the defense of the gospel (v. 16)
—manner of life worthy of the gospel (v. 27a)
—striving for the faith of the gospel (v. 27b)

When referring to the deep bond of Christian love that he had for his friends at Philippi, Paul reminds them of the framework of his concern for them. This Christian love that he has for them is found in the truth of the gospel, and this same gospel must be stated, confirmed, defended, and lived, as the above verses indicate. When viewed in this perspective, therefore, the activity involved in the defense of the gospel becomes a wholly natural and vital activity, not separated from Christian doctrine and life, but interwoven with them. By stressing defense in verses 7 and 16 of Philippians 1, Paul shows its importance. The Christian's ethical behavior, with the major issue of consistency of life, flows naturally from the truth contained in the Good News, the gospel of Jesus Christ (v. 27). Paul thus shows a biblical balance in the close interrelationship seen in Philippians 1 between Christian conduct, communication, and clarification (defense) of answers to questions raised about the person and/or message of the Christian herald. Seen in this relationship, therefore, the matter of defense is an integral part of the entire Christian enterprise.

The apostle Peter wrote, "But sanctify Christ as Lord in your hearts, always *being* ready to make a defense [*apologia*] to every one who asks you to give an account for the hope that is in you, yet with gentleness and reverence" (1 Peter 3:15). A word of caution is definitely in order as this passage is examined. It is an oversimplification to lift this verse out of its context and place it at the focal point of a book about the defense of the Christian position. The verse functions in a context that was particularly meaningful for readers in the first century. Doubtless in Peter's usage there was a broad spectrum of activity implied in the word *apologia* and an equally broad spectrum of occasions in which this kind of activity was to take place. However, on the basis that all Scripture has a teaching content and a vital applicatory message, believers living in any century of the Christian era can find principles here that will govern the activity of apologetics. It certainly specifies that one must be ready to give a careful answer to issues involving the Christian hope. This hope is linked with the theological verities of the Christian faith, implying certainty and a fixed object of faith. The readiness to give a cogent statement of defense stressed in this verse clearly implies preparation on the part of the one who is to give the statement. This preparation would logically involve a knowledge both of the position being defended and of the attacks brought against it. Along with an awareness of these issues, the apostle Peter stresses an attitude of dependence on God. Very simply, this passage calls for both the act of giving a defense and an attitude in this activity of total dependence on God. The biblical meekness stressed is certainly not weakness but rather strength governed by the discipline of a controlled spirit on the part of the one doing the answering. The passage teaches that believers are to be prepared to give an answer, but this answer or defense is to be devoid of all arrogance and pride or self-sufficiency.

Some scholars have felt that 1 Peter 3:15 has no bearing on the defense of the faith in modern times. They feel that this verse must be limited to the times of persecution faced by the readers in the first century, when believers were called on to give a specific legal and formal defense to the Roman world power. Passages in the book, such as 1 Peter 2:13–17, are cited to help give credibility to this viewpoint. The conclusion is thus drawn that 1 Peter 3:15 implies only a technical answer or legal defense in the face of immediate confrontation with the Roman government. However, Alan M. Stibbs evaluates this position in the following manner:

> The accompanying phraseology in this verse, however, combines forcibly to suggest something which might be called for at any time in the most informal and spontaneous manner. The verb *aitein, asketh,* suggests ordinary conversation rather than an official enquiry. The words *always* and *to every man* make the reference completely general and comprehensive. The Christian must remember that anybody at any time may ask him to explain and justify his Christian confidence. . . . The Christian is then to engage, not in an aggressive attack on the other person's will or prejudice, but in a logical account (the word translated *reason* is *logos*), or reasoned explanation of the hope that is distinctive of

the Christian community (cf. Heb. x. 23, RV). He ought, also, to do it *with meekness and fear*, i.e., without arrogance or self-assertion, with due respect and deference towards men, and with proper awe and reverence before God.[3]

Another important Greek word is the verb *apologeomai*, which means to give a defense in response to charges.[4] Some usages of this verb in the New Testament have a vital bearing on the study of apologetics. In Acts 24:10 Paul set the tone for his response to his attackers, saying, "I cheerfully make my defense [*apologeomai*]." In making his defense Paul deliberately sorted out the charges brought against him and his position and responded in a spirit of dignity. The attitude marking Paul's defense is characterized by the word *euthumōs*, "cheerfully," an adverb based on the adjective *euthumos*, good spirit.[5] The adjective means cheerful or in good spirits and is used to indicate an activity resulting in encouraging someone. This is highly significant in attempting to detect principles from the New Testament that will guide anyone giving a response or an apology. Paul's attitude is not one of condemnation of his critics, but rather one of deep concern for the truth and for the issues of clarification of the matter at hand.

Interestingly, the charges enumerated in Acts 24:5–9 formed the pattern of attack brought against the Christian position for many decades after the apostolic age. Three main charges are in view: sedition against the state (v. 5a), sectarianism with reference to Judaism, and sacrilege against the God of Israel.[6] Paul's straightforward answer amounted to a categorical and factual denial of sedition (24:11–13). Furthermore, he defined the Christian position very concisely as being not a sect, but the pathway of true service to the God of Israel (vv. 14–16). Finally, he described in minute detail his activity in Jerusalem, and he insisted rightfully that it was not sacrilegious (vv. 17–21).

Acts 26:1–2 reveals the use of the Greek verb *apologeomai* as follows: "Paul stretched out his hand and *proceeded* to make his defense [*apologeomai*]. . . . I consider myself fortunate, King Agrippa, that I am about to make my defense [*apologeomai*]." In the ensuing verses, Luke records a Christocentric statement from Paul, who adroitly bases the defense on a major proclamation of the Christian message. The key to his apology seems to be found in verse 22, where he candidly responds to Judaism by noting that the Christian position is an unfolding of what the Old Testament had stated about the Messiah.

BIBLICAL PASSAGES RELATED TO APOLOGETICS

In addition to the key words just studied, there are complete passages of Scripture that establish the validity of the activity of defending the Christian faith. Thus an appeal that makes the defense of the faith a crucial action for believers is recorded in Jude 3: "Beloved, while I was making every effort to write you about our common salvation, I felt the necessity to write to you appealing that you contend earnestly for the faith which was once for all delivered to the saints." The phrase that concerns the student of apologetics is "contend earnestly [epagōnizomai] for the faith." The first readers of these words shared the common salvation that Jude mentions in the earlier part of the verse. This common salvation was based on the redeeming grace of God that had been proclaimed to them in the preaching of the gospel. Now Jude urges these Christians, because of the imminent danger of specific teaching directed against the gospel, to contend earnestly for the faith once for all delivered over to the believers. Unquestionably Jude states that there is a body of teaching known as "the faith" and that this body of teaching has been entrusted to the believers. Furthermore, this entire system of truth was now called into question by false teachers. Jude urges his readers to strive earnestly for (literally, to agonize for) the faith. The background for this word picture is found in the world of athletic games. The athlete "agonizes," or really contends, for a prize; he struggles to win the victory in the event in which he is participating. This activity, of course, implies diligent training and a determined effort to triumph over the other competitors. When we transfer this idea to the concept of Christian warfare, the word picture becomes more vivid. Many false views are being offered to the churches, said Jude. The Christian is to respond diligently to these false views by gaining the victory or mastery over them. Contending for the faith, in other words, functions within a context of careful and calculated study of the opposition and is a determined effort to express and vindicate the

Christian faith so as to fully respond to the opposing positions. Jude 3, therefore, is an important verse, for it enunciates a principle for all ages of the history of the defense of Christianity.

Jude 22 adds another element to this work of defense. Whereas Jude 3 enunciates the general principle of striving for the faith, verse 22 explores the attitude of the defender as he or she engages in the activity of giving defense. The defender's attitude is projected as follows: "And have mercy on some, who are doubting" (v. 22). There is some question as to the wording of the original text here. However, the words of George Lawlor show the bearing of the verse on the study of the defense of the faith:

> It thus seems reasonable to take Jude's admonition to mean that we are to extend mercy to those who may have leanings toward such things as are taught by apostates but who are hesitating in doubt. . . . It may well be that some of them are still hesitating, wavering, in doubt as to what is right or wrong and have taken no final step. Some may be disputatious, to be sure, and under the influence of the apostasy, and attempt to support claims made by apostates. In either case, and in both instances, we must make every effort to correct their mistaken views and impressions, even to the point of rebuke if need be.[7]

Titus 1:9–11 also is a passage to be considered. The immediate context, of course, refers to a description of traits that are to characterize leadership in the church. The elder or overseer sets the pace for the rest of the group in the matter of "holding fast the faithful word which is in accordance with the teaching, that he may be able both to exhort in sound doctrine and to refute those who contradict" (v. 9). The phrase "those who contradict" receives further clarification in verses 10–11. It seems fairly clear that non-Christian positions are in view here, for those involved are teaching false ideas and are viewed as being unidentified with the believers. Paul refers to these very individuals as those "who must be silenced" (v. 11). In this vivid terminology the apostle clearly indicates that the false ideas must be met openly and a response made so that the opposition will be definitely and clearly answered. Even if the words of verse 14 might imply the inclusion of believers, nonetheless the kind of activity being assumed here is that which will be useful to responding to the false ideas as well as clarifying the true position.

We have considered some biblical passages that supply principles for the work of defending the Christian faith. A fitting summary will be to see how Paul in 2 Timothy 2:24–25 addresses this matter of giving a defense of Christian truth. Certainly, anyone who is involved in the vital work of defending the faith needs to follow the example set by these words: "And the Lord's bond-servant must not be quarrelsome, but be kind to all, able to teach, patient when wronged, with gentleness correcting those who are in opposition, if perhaps God may grant them repentance leading to the knowledge of the truth." Workers in this field of defending the faith must be characterized by the qualities set forth in this passage. A perfect balance of human responsibility on the part of the worker and the gracious action of God is given in the last part of 2 Timothy 2:25. A word of correction and clarification must be given, and then God will graciously work in finalizing this word to the end that the change of mind (repentance) is seen as part of His gracious action.

DEFINITIONS AND DISTINCTIONS

Apologetics may be defined as the *clarification and defense of the total system of biblical Christianity with reference to specific attacks against the total system, or with reference to selective attacks against one or more of the basic elements inherent within the system.* Any definition of this subject will naturally reflect the method and approach of the one who gives it. It would seem apparent, however, that certain elements are present in any definition given for this field of study.

First, there is certainly a core of truth to be defended and clarified. The first part of the definition refers to this core. It is not the task of apologetics to state or systematize this biblical core. A detailed statement of Christian theology issues from the work of systematic theology and includes the major facets of our historic Christian Trinitarian position.

Second, there is an ever-changing and yet ever-growing body of data assembled by opponents who bring attacks against the Christian faith. A study of apologetics ideally should equip us to formulate a method of response to any system that sets itself over against the Christian faith. It is helpful to consider at the outset of our study, however, that many of the objections raised against

Christian truth even in the present day have had a long ideological history, and these objections have prompted a careful Christian response from past generations of able defenders of the faith.

Third, separate treatment is demanded by some of the issues in the broad spectrum of subjects included in Christian apologetics. The last part of the definition given for apologetics reflects this factor. For example, a major part of Christian theology deals with the work of our Creator-God in His massive activity of bringing into being all the galaxy systems and all of the various forms of life on earth. Christian theology in the unfolding of the work of creation by God builds on a model of origins that starts with the miraculous work of God. Naturally, this clashes with a model of origins that postulates no personal God but rather assumes a mechanism of chance for the arrival of life. Thus one entire issue of Christian apologetics deals with the Christian position concerning the origin of all things. The dimension of the problem demands that entire volumes be devoted to this one field, even though it is actually only one of the basic elements inherent within the entire Christian position.

Drawing from the Bible key words considered earlier, we can now see how the term *apologetics* can be used in a positive and biblical manner. A given speech in defense is an *apology* in this technical sense of the term. *Apologetics* embraces the entire field of defense and is basic to any individual *apology* or statement in response to specific objections. Admittedly, this is somewhat of an idealistic concept; it involves the building of a system of Christian defense and then the giving of individual "apologies" as objections are articulated. It is like the ideal relationship that should exist between "homiletics," a study of the great principles of sermon building and delivery, and a "sermon," a specific proclamation of biblical truth based on the help and teachings contained in the science of homiletics. By comparison, what a given sermon ideally is to homiletics as a field of study, a given defense statement or apology ideally is to the entire realm of apologetics as a field of study.

There is a close relationship between Christian apologetics and the study of philosophy. At this point someone may be thinking, "Why not simply state the facts of history on which Christianity rests in answering objections and avoid all this speculative reasoning and dialogue with philosophy?" This is a reasonable question. However, as soon as you use the words "facts of history," you are involved already in stating a view about reality, or a framework in which these facts will function, an interpretation of these facts. Interpretation rests on a way of looking at all of reality, and, very simply, the way a person looks at all of reality is his or her "philosophy" of life, or view of life. It is safe to say that most of the objections brought to bear against the Christian position rest on an interpretation, a way of looking at reality, or a philosophy of life that is opposed to Christianity. Thus to understand the objection and to give a better and more cogent response to it, we must attempt to understand the position on which the objection rests. In our response we can then exemplify the spirit and meaning of Jude 3 as discussed earlier.

Philosophy seeks to answer the basic questions of life in various areas of thought. Thus the metaphysician asks, What is reality? The epistemologist asks, How can reality be known, and what can we know? The ethicist asks, What is proper and/or meaningful behavior, or right and wrong, in the light of the reality that can be known? The aesthetician asks, What can be judged the beautiful within the scope of reality?

The Christian realizes that the correct position on all of reality is found in the system of truth revealed in Scripture. Starting with that groundwork or system, which is openly verifiable to all, the Christian can find the ultimate answers to the questions raised by philosophy. Specifically stated, Christian theology gives us the groundwork or basic ingredients on which we formulate specifically Christian answers to the problem areas in the spectrum of philosophy. For example, metaphysics is the study of ultimate reality, or the very nature of being itself. A thoroughly consistent Christian view of metaphysics can be built and articulated on the solid ground of Christian theism. Building on this foundation, the Christian apologete then contrasts this view with false views of metaphysics and points out the inconsistencies of the views that oppose Christianity. All of this can be put into focus with these words:

> It is apparent from this that if we would really defend Christianity as a historical religion we must at the same time defend the theism upon which Christianity is based. This involves us in philosophical discus-

sion. To interpret a fact of history involves a philosophy of history. But a philosophy of history is at the same time a philosophy of reality as a whole. Thus we are driven to philosophical discussion all the time and everywhere.[8]

CONCLUSION

Apologetics is a worthy and fruitful discipline in a Christian curriculum. Although the Bible does not spell out in detail the task or methods of apologetics, nonetheless there are enough passages to indicate that the kind of work done in this field is grounded in principles of Scripture. Every succeeding generation of Christians is called on to give a vital expression of the Christian position. Each generation must also maintain the massive system of Christian Trinitarian orthodoxy on the one hand and to respond to attacks brought against it on the other hand, all the while exemplifying the spirit of Christ and speaking in the power of the risen Savior.

REVIEW QUESTIONS

1. Why have some Christians felt that a study of apologetics is a waste of time?
2. What New Testament word (noun) lies behind our term *apologetics,* and what does it mean?
3. How does Philippians 1 show that the defense of the gospel is vitally related to Christian doctrine and life?
4. What does 1 Peter 3:15 suggest by way of application for giving defense?
5. What specific reasons can be given to show that 1 Peter 3:15 relates to a general statement of defense for any situation, rather than a specific response only to an official trial or inquiry?
6. What principles for the work of apologetics can be drawn from Jude 3?
7. How specifically do the terms *apologetics* and *apology* relate?
8. How do philosophy and apologetics relate as fields of study and work?

FOR FURTHER READING

Killen, R. Allen. "Apologetics." In *Wycliffe Bible Encyclopedia,* vol. 2, edited by C. F. Pfeiffer, H. F. Vos, John Rea. Chicago: Moody, 1975.

Lewis, Gordon R. "The Problem of Testing Christianity's Truth-Claims." Chap. 1 in *Testing Christianity's Truth-Claims: Approaches to Christian Apologetics.* Chicago: Moody, 1976.

Ramm, Bernard. "Apologetics." In *Baker's Dictionary of Theology*, edited by E. F. Harrison. Grand Rapids: Baker, 1960.

_____. "Brief Introduction to Christian Apologetics.' Chap. 1 in *Varieties of Christian Apologetics*. Rev. ed. Grand Rapids: Baker, 1961.

_____. "The Nature and Function of Christian Apologetics." Chap. 1 in *The God Who Makes a Difference: A Christian Appeal to Reason*. Waco: Word, 1972.

Warfield, Benjamin B. "Apologetics." In *The New Schaff-Herzog Encyclopedia of Religious Knowledge*, vol. 1, edited by S. M. Jackson et al. New York: Funk and Wagnalls, 1908-11.

CHAPTER 2

Apologetics
and Evangelism

Every Christian is called upon to give a vital witness to the saving grace of God as revealed in the gospel of Jesus Christ and to share his or her faith with others. There is also clear evidence, as was seen from the discussion concerning 1 Peter 3:15, that believers should be able to give a response to challenges brought against their faith. This kind of response is the kind of activity fostered by apologetics. It is imperative now that the relationship between the two vital fields of apologetics and evangelism be studied closely and systematically.

Regardless of the particular system of apologetics held, it appears that many apologetes find little or no difference between the work of evangelism and that of apologetics.[1] For all practical purposes, evangelism and apologetics become virtually identified. If, in contrast to this, a careful distinction between these two realms is maintained, the proper strength and place of each activity are preserved.

THE PRIMARY TASK OF EVANGELISM

Evangelism is simply proclaiming the good news of the gospel of Jesus Christ. The Greek word *euangelizomai* and its cognates are central to this activity. The word means to "announce good news . . . of the divine message of salvation, the Messianic proclamation, the gospel."[2] The activity involved in evangelism has been very carefully set forth in the following description:

Evangelization refers to the initial phase of Christian ministry. It is the authoritative proclamation of the gospel of Jesus Christ as revealed in the Bible in relevant and intelligible terms, in a persuasive manner with the definite purpose of making Christian converts. It is a presentation–penetration–permeation–confrontation that not only elicits but demands a decision. It is preaching the gospel of Jesus Christ for a verdict.[3]

Both the activity involved in and the aims set for evangelism must be grounded in the Word of God. James I. Packer writes:

According to the New Testament, evangelism is just preaching the gospel, the evangel. It is a work of communication in which Christians make themselves mouthpieces for God's message of mercy to sinners. Anyone who faithfully delivers that message, under whatever circumstances . . . is evangelizing. Since the divine message finds its climax in a plea from the Creator to a rebel world to turn and put faith in Christ, the delivering of it involves the summoning of one's hearers to conversion. If you are not, in this sense, seeking to bring about conversions, you are not evangelizing; this we have seen already. But the way to tell whether in fact you are evangelizing is not to ask whether conversions are known to have resulted from your witness. It is to ask whether you are faithfully making known the gospel message.[4]

Thus evangelism centers in the proclamation of the gospel of Jesus Christ. Every generation of Christians since the apostolic age has faced the challenge of obeying Christ's words in the Great Commission as stated in Matthew 28:18–20 and thereby being vitally involved in evangelism.

SOME CONTRASTS BETWEEN
EVANGELISM AND APOLOGETICS

A Contrast in Description

Several rather striking contrasts between evangelism and apologetics become apparent on reflection. First, one observes a major contrast in the very description or definition of each activity. Evangelism is primarily the *communication* of the gospel of Jesus Christ. Apologetics, however, involves the *clarification* of the entire Christian position on which the gospel rests. An ideal pattern of Christian activity puts evangelism first, followed by apologetics. Hearers are first given a clear statement of the gospel (as cogently delineated, for example, in 1 Corinthians 15:1–11). This presentation is then followed up with a response to questions, or even dialogue, about different viewpoints that in some way challenge the gospel or the entire Christian position on which the gospel rests. This response seems to fit naturally into a pattern of clarification that takes place after the primary task of confronting individuals with the gospel. However, one must be careful at this point not to oversimplify the matter. The same spirit that caused the apostle Paul to agonize for his friends outside of Christ must prevail in the minds of those giving a detailed apology to objections raised against facets of Christian truth. Paul indicated the proper emphasis here when he wrote the famous words of 1 Corinthians 9:22: "To the weak I become weak, that I might win the weak; I have become all things to all men, that I may by all means save some."

An example might help to clarify this distinction further. When a Christian cites, for instance, the biblical evidence for the virgin birth of Christ in response to questions raised from the viewpoint of a philosophy that can permit no such happening in its concept of the universe, he is giving an *apology* for the truth. Naturally, this process involves a clear biblical statement and a faithful use of the reasoning process flowing from the biblical evidence. This work is primarily related to the sphere of apologetics. Specifically, in the immediate context of this work, as the believer answers objections to the truth of the Virgin Birth, he is not at this point proclaiming the gospel, that is, he is not directly evangelizing the critic. However, the mental and spiritual attitude of the defender should parallel Paul's attitude as expressed in 1 Corinthians 9:22. In other words, even in giving a defense, we should not step outside ourselves, so to speak, and become detached from our place as servants of Christ and witnesses to the saving action of God's grace in Jesus Christ. A determined and thoughtful recognition of this need will guard against an arid and speculative argumentation that fails to relate to the person who espouses the non-Christian system. Thus it is important for the biblically oriented apologete to remember that giving answers designed to defend the faith is not the same thing as explaining the gospel to gain converts in evangelism.

In summary, this first distinction must be preserved. Evangelistic activity involves the clear-cut statement of the Christian gospel, a veritable confrontation of the world with the truth of the Christian message. Apologetical activity involves a careful statement in response to any objections that are raised. Within this first distinction there is an implicit result for each activity. In evangelism the activity is aimed at eliciting a response to the gospel in keeping, certainly, with the work of God. In other words the persuasive element is seen here, together with the result of seeing God at work in opening the heart to the truth of the gospel (cf. Acts 16:14) so that evangelism reaches a climactic fruition. By contrast, apologetical activity functions in giving answers and in perhaps clarifying misunderstandings or false ideas held by non-Christians concerning the truth. The climax of apologetics would seem to be in finding fulfillment when the answer is given and the case for Christianity is stated. Then the truth is opened up, so to speak, for investigation and further confrontation.

A Contrast in Data

Second, there is a contrast in the data involved in each field. Evangelism primarily involves the gospel. In 1 Corinthians 15:1–2a, and also in verses 3–11, the apostle Paul carefully sets forth the gospel. The Good News centers around the basic truths enunciated in 1 Corinthians 15:3–4: "For I delivered to you as of first importance what I also received, that Christ died for our sins according to the Scriptures, and that He was buried, and that He was raised on the third day according to the Scriptures."

Here is the core of the apostolic preaching. This message, often called the *kerygma*, rests on a foundation of great truths of the Christian Trinitarian position. In other words it is a theological message arising out of a theological system. Sometimes the objections or onslaughts from non-Christian speculative systems are directed against truths proclaimed in the gospel itself. However, many times these objections are raised against the Christian system on which the gospel rests. Thus apologetical activity is not limited simply to the changeless message of the gospel itself but also embraces the whole spectrum of truth that is timeless and foundational to the gospel. The contrast here can be seen by comparing Jude 3 with 1 Corinthians

15:3–4. As a discipline apologetics must defend the entire Christian faith, the "faith which was once for all delivered," as Jude 3 puts it. Evangelism, as a discipline, involves the data strictly pertinent to the gospel.

A Contrast in Demands

Third, there is a difference in the demands placed on workers in evangelism compared to the demands in apologetics. The work of the evangelist ideally is to present the gospel message, a message viewed in Scripture as a sacred trust (Titus 1:3). The Good News is to be preached without any change from the original gospel message proclaimed by the apostles. Perhaps the well-worn cliché "changeless truth for changing times" has been overworked, but it is certainly true. Workers in evangelism in each succeeding generation should constantly seek effective communication, but they must not change the message, the evangel.

Apologetics of necessity will involve a *changing* response to changing attacks. Long ago, for example, certain systems of speculative thought raised objections to aspects of the Christian position. Faithful Christian defenders of that era worked with those issues and provided suitable responses to them. As time passed, many of those older systems of thought passed off the scene. Today newer systems have arisen, and Christians need to respond to them in contending earnestly for the faith. Thus the faith stands changeless as a sacred trust that God deposited in the apostolic proclamation. The answers change, based on a discerning understanding of the systems from which the questions are given. The words of a defender of the faith of many years ago are pertinent by way of illustration:

> It is evident, also, that the mode in which Apologetics shall undertake and best discharge its task will vary from age to age. As already indicated, the redeeming activity is always essentially the same, but the circumstances in which it is exhibited are subject to change. This naturally requires that Apologetics should be prepared to show how fully Christianity is qualified for every emergency in the conflict. Hence Apologetics must be ever watchful and ready to discern the signs of the times. In this service, to be forewarned is often to be forearmed. The assault may now be at one point, and again at another. Hence, Apologetics must be always alert, and ready for the foe at every

turn; for the defences of one age may not suit another, and the vindication which served at one time may not be sufficient for another.[5]

Table 1[6] summarizes the areas of contrast between evangelism
and apologetics.

TABLE 1

	EVANGELISM	APOLOGETICS
Source	All Christians	Any given Christian, only when specific objection is raised to the truth
Content	Primarily, the gospel (kerygma)	Ultimately, the whole biblical Trinitarian system, including kerygma and didache (teaching)
Sphere	Universal (Acts 1:8— anyplace, anytime)	Somewhat more limited; in the sphere of response to challenge (1 Peter 3:15)
Reason	Obedience to the command of Christ (Matt. 28:18–20; Acts 1:8)	For the defense of the Christian system; in obedience to the Word of God (Jude 3)
Method	In full dependence on the Holy Spirit (Phil. 4:13)	In full dependence on the Holy Spirit (Phil. 4:13)
Operation	Confrontation, an all-out effort to state the biblical gospel	Clarification; an all-out effort to clarify the body of truth known as the Christian Trinitarian system
Expected Results	Acceptance of Jesus Christ as personal Sin-Bearer and Savior (Acts 16:14); invitation received	Articulation of the truth; possible correction of misunderstandings about salient features of the system; possible basis for further contact; vindication stated

SUMMARY AND CONCLUSION

Apologetics and evangelism do have some significant differ-
ences. The two fields of activity, even by the very nature of the
definition of terms, stand in contrast to each other. Apologetics is
primarily devoted to providing answers, whereas evangelism is de-

voted to proclaiming truth. Also, in the strict sense the two realms deal with different subject matter. Evangelism primarily relates to the *kerygma* or gospel core; apologetics builds on the *didache* or teaching content of the entire Christian position. Furthermore, apologetes will always be developing changing analyses and answers to opposing positions; in contrast, proclaimers of the Good News will conscientiously strive to avoid any change in the message, even though attempting to state it carefully in relationship to the problems of any period of time in history. Certainly the attitude of the Christian in giving answers, or in doing the work of apologetics, should be one of deep concern for the person and system bringing the objection.

This attitude is reflected in the earnest appeal that Paul made to King Agrippa. Agrippa's words seem at best to contain very little positive indication of response to Paul's message (Acts 26:28). Nonetheless, the apostle refers to all his hearers, including any who would bring reasoned objections to the truth of his message (v. 29). The latter verse indicates Paul's desire that all might have the same relationship to the Lord Jesus Christ that he had. The apostle's ministry in Acts 26 serves as a pattern for the study of the close interrelationship between apologetics and evangelism. Paul was actually giving a defense of his own person and message. He not only carefully answered the charges brought against him but also proclaimed the message of Christian truth.

We can be sure, even as Paul was sure, that God the Holy Spirit works sovereignly as an individual hears the gospel proclaimed in biblical evangelism. The same Holy Spirit likewise works sovereignly as an individual listens to a presentation of the defense of the faith by a biblical apologete. At this point we must be careful not to limit God! God may be pleased to use the information provided in response to questions as a probing instrument to arouse interest in the things pertaining to Christ. In evangelizing one brings a message, and God opens the heart to the truth (Acts 16:14). In apologetics the apologete answers deep questions raised about the entire Christian position or facets of it, and, again, God calls people to faith (Acts 17:34).

Many apologetes note that there is a kind of "pre-evangelism" function that can be accomplished by the kind of arguments and responses given from apologetics. This fact is vividly illustrated in the fascinating account of the conversion of Viggo B. Olsen, M.D., as recorded in his book *Daktar, Diplomat in Bangladesh*. Dr. and Mrs. Olsen, prior to their becoming Christians, engaged in a studious and concerted effort to refute Christianity. Their program of study and searching gives ample proof of the interrelationship of apologetics and evangelism but also the distinctiveness of each field. In giving answers to the Olsens' objections, believers provided them with books that dealt very specifically with the kind of arguments found in Christian apologetics. Especially pertinent to our discussion here are chapters 5 and 6 of the book by Olsen, who states:

> These and other books engaged our minds as Joan and I simultaneously sought to find error in the Christian Scriptures. Christian evidences claimed that the Christian faith is not a blind faith based on imaginary ideas but a true and living faith based on historical fact and a very large amount of valid evidence. We doubted it and fought it but kept reading.[7]

During all their period of searching diligently and of reading books on evidences and apologetics, the Olsens were obviously not believers in Christ. Yet they engaged in a process of thinking and reflecting on the kind of argumentation that is used in apologetics. God graciously worked in their minds and hearts, and they ultimately trusted Christ as their own personal Sin-Bearer and Mediator. The truth they gradually learned to *appreciate* concerning the total Christian position and its firm stance on objective truth was the very same truth that they came to *appropriate* in the decision they made to believe in the Lord Jesus Christ.

The defender of the faith is not necessarily expecting the unregenerate person to agree with the arguments or answers. This fact, however, should not keep the believer from speaking back, in a spirit of Christian concern, to the objector. As amply illustrated in the case of the Olsens, the same processes of thought operating in the mind of an unregenerate person who gives expression to objections to Christianity are also operating to enable that person to hear the response of the Christian, or to read that response in works of apologetics. God will work in this process as He Himself is pleased so to work. He can use this kind of process of answering objections to glorify Himself and to penetrate the thinking of the individual. Again, in all this activity the believer functions under the guidelines of Paul's striking words in Philippians 4:13: "I can do all things [including giving a witness or making a defense] through Him who strengthens me."

REVIEW QUESTIONS

1. What is the primary task of evangelism?
2. Contrast apologetics and evangelism as to the description of each field.
3. How can the Christian guard against an attitude of speculation and argumentation in giving a defense?
4. What exact truths are involved in presenting the gospel?
5. Why does apologetic activity include more than the gospel?
6. Contrast concisely apologetics and evangelism as to the data pertinent to each field.
7. Contrast apologetics and evangelism as to the demands placed on workers in each realm.
8. What is the use of speaking back to objectors in defense of the faith if we are not sure that they will agree with our arguments or answers?

FOR FURTHER READING

Packer, James I. *Evangelism and the Sovereignty of God.* Downers Grove, Ill.: InterVarsity, 1961. Chap. 3.

Peters, George W. *A Biblical Theology of Missions.* Chicago: Moody, 1972. Chap. 1.

Schaeffer, Francis A. "Section V—Pre-Evangelism: No Soft Option" (pp. 139–47). In *The God Who Is There.* Downers Grove, Ill.: InterVarsity, 1968.

Warfield, Benjamin, B. "Introduction to Francis R. Beattie's *Apologetics.* In *Selected Shorter Writings of Benjamin B. Warfield—II,* edited by John E. Meeter. 2 vols. Nutley, N.J.: Presbyterian and Reformed, 1970, 1973.

CHAPTER 3

The Defense of the Faith in the New Testament— Selected Patterns and Principles

Scripture provides some examples of how believers during the apostolic age responded to world views or systems that opposed the Christian position. A word of caution is in order as this study takes shape. We must avoid reading into Scripture our ideas and our thought-forms about apologetics, or any other activity for that matter, as we study some biblical case histories of how Christians dealt with the issue of opposition to the Christian faith. The purpose of this investigation will be to extract the timeless principles that the Christian defender was following so that we can use these same principles when we face ideologies that oppose the Christian system today.

STEPHEN'S DEFENSE IN ACTS 7

The first case study is the masterful speech delivered by Stephen in Acts 7. All the ingredients for a true defense are here. The charges brought against the Christian messenger and his message are listed in Acts 6:11. Apparently Stephen had consistently and openly proclaimed the message that Jesus is the Messiah. As F. F. Bruce notes:

> Stephen's reasoning provoked keen opposition, and a full-dress debate was probably arranged. The exact subject of the debate is not stated; it no doubt concerned the Messiahship of Jesus, but Stephen expounded the implications of His Messiahship more radically than his fellow-believers had hitherto expounded it.[1]

Several factors make this a fascinating introduction to the defense of the faith. First, Luke mentions the place of the initial contact with the opposition: "But some men from what was called the Synagogue of the Freedmen, *including* both Cyrenians and Alexandrians, and some from Cilicia and Asia, rose up and argued with Stephen" (Acts 6:9). Since Saul of Tarsus came from this region of Cilicia, it seems logical to think that perhaps he himself would have had occasion to hear Stephen. Whether this was the case or not, it is certain that the Christian message was proclaimed with power and wisdom. It was then attacked, for Acts 6:9 clearly states that the message was understood and then an attempt was made to refute it. The result of this initial confrontation is then described: "And *yet* they were unable to cope with the wisdom and the Spirit with which he was speaking" (v. 10). The Bible clearly indicates that the contact between Stephen and these challengers was persistent and continued. The Greek word for "argued" in verse 9 is *suzētountes,* and its tense and meaning clearly imply a continuing disputation, a question-and-answer type of dialogue. A. T. Robertson gives the following helpful comment:

> Present active participle of *sunzēteō,* to question together as the two on the way to Emmaus did (Luke 24:15). Such interruptions were common with Jews. They give a skilled speaker great opportunity for reply if he is quick in repartee. Evidently Stephen was fully equipped for the emergency. One of their synagogues had men from Cilicia in it, making it practically certain that young Saul of Tarsus, the brilliant student of Gamaliel, was present and tried his wits with Stephen. His ignominious defeat may be one explanation of his zest in the stoning of Stephen (Acts 8:1).[2]

The graphic portrayal of this defense of the faith given by Luke the historian in Acts clearly implies that Stephen met the challenge they brought with careful and analytical thought; moreover, he stated the case so cogently in the power of the Holy Spirit that they could not answer it. Thus they invented false charges and set the stage for the *apologia* given in Acts 7.

The case against Christianity is stated in Acts 6:13–14. It is actually a misrepresentation of the Christian position, being couched in words that would seek to align the Jewish populace against the

Christian messengers. Put simply, the attack against Christianity suggests that the messenger, Stephen, spoke against both the holy temple in Jerusalem and the entire way of life of Judaism as epitomized in the way of Moses and the customs of Judaism (Acts 6:14).

The case for Christianity is stated clearly and distinctly in Acts 7:1–53. Its obvious significance for apologetics is noted as follows:

> Such a speech as this was by no means calculated to secure an acquittal before the Sanhedrin. It is rather a defence of pure Christianity as God's appointed way of worship; Stephen here shows himself to be the precursor of the later Christian apologists, especially those who defended Christianity against Judaism.[3]

Briefly, Stephen states his position with telling logic and force. The true core of worship that should be offered up to the sovereign God of Israel is spiritual, not material. God had never limited Himself or His own Self-revelation to one place or time. Stephen skillfully gives a panoramic sweep of Israel's history with the purpose of showing that the God of the ages can and did manifest Himself to Joseph, Móses, and Abraham long before the building of the temple in Jerusalem. Stephen continued his defense with the assured truth enunciated in Acts 7:48: "The Most High does not dwell in *houses* made by *human* hands." The method of Stephen was to review God's revelation of Himself in history and Israel's stubborn response to that revelation. The coming "Righteous One," Jesus of Nazareth, was the real source and instrument of the knowledge of the Most High God. The prophets had announced His coming (v. 52). The heritage of the rejection of God's messengers all through Israel's history culminated in the present generation of Stephen's attackers. In fact, Stephen deliberately and even calculatingly links their refusal to accept the truth about Messiah with the line of rejection traced all the way back to those who repudiated Moses (v. 40) and to those who persecuted the prophets (v. 52).

Stephen clearly stated the case and his implication is obvious. Through the insight and wisdom granted by the Holy Spirit, Stephen understood the truth implied in the entire Christian mission. The introduction of Christianity meant the end of temple worship, for God had reaffirmed His dealings with people on the basis of His own

Self-revelation progressively unfolded in the Old Testament and epitomized in "the Righteous One," Jesus, the Christ of God.

Today the context of apologetics is radically different from what it was when Stephen set forth his case. Nevertheless, one major timeless principle that stands out from Stephen's example allows a defender of the faith in any century to draw insight and help. Put concisely, it is this: in any defense of the Christian position, a careful attempt must be made to function within the strengthening work of the Holy Spirit. Interaction with this principle must not be avoided by viewing it as merely pious talk or dismissing it as completely irrelevant in the give-and-take of real debate. The repeated emphasis of the text of Scripture is that Stephen's lifestyle was characterized as being full of wisdom and of the Holy Spirit. While there are various implications for the Christian life in the entire area of the fullness of the Spirit, there are also implications for a consistent defense of the faith. This is not to suggest that the enabling of the Holy Spirit in this endeavor will assure instant success or instant validation of the claims made in a confrontation between the defender of the faith and one who raises objections. It is simply a recognition that a consistent and honest attempt must be made to invite the strengthening One, the Holy Spirit, into the entire perspective of defense; by so doing the defender fulfills another biblical guideline found in these words: "I can do all things through Him who strengthens me" (Phil. 4:13). Certainly, no one would care to insist that giving a careful statement of defense does not come under the purview of the "all things" in this verse! Thus by giving thoughtful and concentrated attention to this truth, the defender of the faith can speak in the power of the Spirit, even as did Stephen in his great statement recorded in Acts 7.

PAUL'S DEFENSE WITH REFERENCE TO JUDAISM: MESSIAH AND CRUCIFIXION

Another deep-seated objection arose against the Christian message in the apostolic age. Stemming from Judaism, this objection focused on the death by crucifixion of Jesus of Nazareth. This was a "stumbling block" to the Jews, as 1 Corinthians 1:23 indicates. Bruce states the problem as follows:

To Jews the crucifixion of Jesus was a formidable obstacle to believing him to be the appointed Messiah; how could the Messiah, on whom the blessing of God rested in a unique degree, have died the death on which the curse of God was expressly pronounced? It was written plainly in the law: "a hanged man is accursed by God" (Deut. 21:23). That Jesus came under the description "a hanged man" was undeniable; but it was blasphemous to suggest that one who clearly was "accursed by God" could be Israel's Messiah.[4]

The groundwork for a Christian response to the charge that the Messiah would surely never succumb to such an ignominious death as death "on a cross" (Acts 5:30; 10:39) is laid in Galatians 3:10–13. There Paul makes a comparison between the judgment of God assigned to all who do not keep the law of God perfectly and the judgment of God assigned to one who hangs on a tree. In this there clearly seems to be a legal or "forensic" equivalent: the curse in one form (death by the cross) is seen in some way as substituting for the curse in another form. By reading Galatians 3:10–13 in close sequence, one cannot help but agree with Bruce, who says:

> Christ, by bearing the curse of God in one form (death by crucifixion), liberated his people who were under that curse in another form (through failure to keep the whole law of God), and secured for them the blessings of the gospel. This solution of the problem may well have taken shape in Paul's mind sooner rather than later in the period following his conversion, as the whole of his thinking became reorientated around a new centre.[5]

This line of defense fits quite readily into the entire work of God in revealing His true righteousness and into His great work of reversing human opinions and attitudes about the Messiah. One of the ministries of the Holy Spirit promised by Jesus was to demonstrate God's true standard of righteousness to the world (John 16:10). Through the seeming paradox of the events of the Cross and the Resurrection, the One whom the entire world looked on as unrighteous and worthy of a criminal's death (John 19:7) was vindicated and actually viewed as "the Holy and Righteous One" (Acts 3:14). Thus a defense of this key issue in Christian truth really involves the clarification and explanation of the death of the Messiah within the entire perspective of God's vantage point, not simply from man's view.

The lesson to be learned and applied to defense activity in any age is that often apologetics will involve simply a strong statement of clarification that opens up the possibilities for an objector to look at the evidence from another angle or perspective. Acceptance of the defense in a believing and trusting manner, naturally, is bound up with God's gracious action in opening the heart. However, it would be taking biblical evidence too far to suggest that there would really be no reason to even make a statement on the grounds that the non-Christian objector will not accept or ultimately understand anything said. There is just too much biblical evidence to the contrary that indicates a level of understanding often is attained by many objectors; the evidence shows that the failure to respond to the defense statement of Christianity usually is the result of deliberate and willful rejection, not faulty understanding or lack of comprehension. It is always true that rejection involves the total person, including the heart, mind, and will. Christian defense always functions within this realm of open acknowledgment of the needs of the total person, and the apologete considers the work of God in bringing to pass His good pleasure in all things.

A CHALLENGE FROM INTELLECTUAL SKEPTICISM: PAUL AT ATHENS

Elements of Paul's address on the Areopagus recorded in Acts 17 can form some fitting guidelines for modern statements defending the real nature of Christian theism. However, one must avoid the danger of building too much modern-day "scaffolding," so to speak, replete with inferences drawn for varied approaches to the field of apologetics, from the great work of Paul in his Athenian proclamation.

At the outset of this discussion we must clearly see that Paul did not introduce the Christian position as only a probable option for these erudite exchangers of information gathered there. Rather, he forthrightly announced certain truths about the God of creation and the Lord of history, and he swiftly concluded that this same God had already appointed Jesus to be the Judge of individuals. Therefore, Acts 17 is not primarily an attempt on the part of Paul to argue these hearers into a relationship with the God of the ages. Rather, it is simply a reasoned response to their inquiry as to the things they had heard about his message. Even with these cautionary points stated, however, we must realize that the example in Acts 17 of a statement of Christian response to a challenge from intellectual skepticism fairly bristles with implications for Christian defense in the modern era.

First, let us notice that the locale of this challenge to Christian truth was significant. Athens had enjoyed political glory in its earlier so-called golden age. However, by the time Paul visited Athens, the city's glory had largely faded. It was at that time a free and allied city within the Roman Empire. Various philosophies or world views had been taught here in this famous city. After all, it was the native city of Socrates and Plato and was the adopted home of Aristotle, Epicurus, and Zeno.

Second, we note the nature of the preparation for this challenge to the gospel message. The apostle Paul was deeply moved as he observed this city with its many temples and images. What today are viewed as masterful works of art and brilliant sculpture were in Paul's day seen additionally as images of pagan deities. Thus the preparation here for this real contact between the Christian herald and the non-Christian inquirers included having a knowledge of both the religious world and the philosophical world.

Third, we observe that the immediate parties involved in this challenge from the world of pagan intellectual thought were the Epicurean and Stoic philosophers (Acts 17:18). The Stoics had as their founder the Cypriot Zeno (340–265 B.C.). They took their name from the painted stoas or porticoes (porchlike structures supported by columns) where Zeno traditionally taught his views in Athens. Apparently the major stress of the Stoics was on a rational outlook on life. Thus a certain reasonable self-sufficiency and even moral earnestness characterized their lifestyle. Their view of deity was certainly foreign to the rich truth of revelation on which Paul's teaching was grounded. To them, "God" was the world-soul, and this position involved them in incipient pantheism. Interpreters of this viewpoint note that the Stoics were marked by a pride that was distinctly built on self-achievement and was diametrically opposed to the spirit of Christianity.

The Epicureans were another of the parties present at Athens. Epicurus (341–270 B.C.) developed an ethical theory based on the understanding of the universe offered by Democritus. It was actually an early atomic theory. In their approach to life the Epicureans gave pleasure the place of priority. However, they understood that the true goal of life was to be free from disturbing passions and fears, and so they advocated that pleasure must be controlled by tranquillity.

It must be noted that in addition to the Epicurean and Stoic philosophers there most likely were many others present to hear the message given by Paul. Clues concerning the rather broad spectrum of vantage points on hand are given in Acts 17:18, 21. Doubtless the predominant group of hearers included bystanders and those who enjoyed hearing the exchange of ideas often presented there.

Fourth, the actual presentation of this challenge to Paul came about in an unusual way. With reference to Paul's own person, some of his challengers asked, "What would this idle babbler wish to say?" (Acts 17:18). The word *babbler* translates the Greek term *spermologos* (literally, "seed picker"). This term was flung at Paul as a very studied insult, possibly with some contemptuousness. It could imply that the Athenians meant Paul resembled a bird picking up seeds as he gleaned scraps, bits and pieces of information from here and there and spread them around in aimless fashion. Possibly the implication was that certainly his ideas would not be worthy of the lofty thoughts of Athenians. With reference to Paul's message, the text of Acts 17:18 pinpoints the proclamation of the central truth of Christian theism: Jesus and the resurrection. What Paul declared included such a stress on these two terms that some scholars feel the hearers caught only the stress on the sound of the two words in the Greek: *Iēsous* (Jesus) and *anastasis* (resurrection). Possibly some of the hearers mistakenly thought Paul was proclaiming two new powers or deities, perhaps the personified powers of *Iasis* (quite similar in sound to *Iēsous*) and *anastasis* and also including the thought of restoration. Bruce has accurately summarized the situation:

> But a man who was introducing a new religion came under the jurisdiction of the court of the Areopagus, so called from its original meeting-place on the Areopagus ("Mars' hill"). This was the most venerable

court in Athens, which enjoyed great prestige because of its antiquity and took specific cognizance of certain moral and religious questions. Before this court, then, Paul was brought—perhaps in the "Painted Colonnade" in the *agora,* which was now its customary meeting-place. He was not required to defend himself as though he were on trial for some offence; he was rather invited to expound his teaching before the body which was responsible to decide whether it contravened public weal or not.[6]

Paul found a point of contact with these hearers: "For while I was passing through and examining the objects of your worship, I also found an altar with this inscription, 'TO AN UNKNOWN GOD.' What therefore you worship in ignorance, this I proclaim to you" (Acts 17:23). Discerning their recognition of ignorance, Paul builds on this contact to set before them the true nature of the God of Scripture. N. B. Stonehouse analyzed this as follows:

> Paul makes the most of their public profession of lack of knowledge concerning the objects of worship by virtually reading it back to them as a characterization of their religion. He says in effect, "That which ye worship *acknowledging openly your ignorance,* I proclaim unto you." The ignorance rather than the worship is thus underscored, and Paul is indicating that he will inform them with regard to that concerning which they acknowledge ignorance.[7]

The vital principle here is that the point of contact for Paul's statement of clarification was *not* a common knowledge of the true God of Scripture that these hearers were encouraged to discover, as if to say that they all along had really worshiped the true God. Far from it! Paul's real principle is that their acknowledged ignorance is to be met with accurate information! Their ignorance rather than their worship is stressed. This is patently clear from the way Luke records the account. He affirms that Paul nowhere links the pagan idol itself to the God of the Bible. Acts 17:23 states this: *"what* therefore you worship in ignorance, *this* I proclaim to you." (italics mine). The italicized words are neuter in gender in the Greek text and specifically guard the truth of the real nature of God. Paul moves *from* the realm of the *truth* that they had constructed an altar to an unknown deity *to* the realm of *truth* and information about the true God.

A few observations on this major presentation of Christian truth are in order. Paul clearly expected these hearers to understand his message and draw correct conclusions from his message, regardless of any presuppositions they had about reality. Actually, Paul simply states the truth about God's nature, providence, creation, and ultimate judgment. He "speaks" these truths right into their thought patterns, so to speak, with no shred of evidence that he expected them to shift ground ideologically or to change their thought patterns or presuppositions in order to understand his message. He states the facts as they are and reveals the correct interpretation of the facts. His appeal moves to the striking conclusion that the God of creation is also the God of judgment. Paul affirms that He will judge the world, offering as proof the historical fact of Christ's resurrection from the dead (Acts 17:31). Paul's method is to state flatly the fact of the resurrection of Christ and to announce the theological pattern of truth that gives meaning to the historical event. The apostle says God raised up Jesus for the actual task of judgment. The information given in verse 31 confirms the need to pay attention to Paul's appeal to repent, as given in verse 30.

In summary, the place of the resurrection of Jesus in the proclamation of Paul is climactic. Acts 17:31 states this: "Because He has fixed a day in which He will judge the world in righteousness through a Man whom He has appointed, having furnished *proof to all* men by raising Him from the dead" (italics mine). The Greek word for "proof" is *pistis*, which often is translated "faith." Commenting on this Greek word, A. T. Robertson noted:

> Whereof he hath given assurance *(pistin paraschōn)*. Second aorist active participle of *parechō*, old verb to furnish, used regularly by Demosthenes for bringing forward evidence. Note this old use of *pistis* as conviction or ground of confidence (Heb. 11:1) like a note or title-deed, a conviction resting on solid basis of fact. All the other uses of *pistis* grow out of this one from *peithō*, to persuade.[8]

The reactions of the audience are cataloged in Acts 17:32. These hearers could not fit this truth into their way of looking at reality! Nothing could be clearer in this passage. The concept of a "resurrection of dead ones" (literal rendering of Acts 17:32a) could not be accepted and placed into their presuppositional framework or way of looking at reality as just another interesting fact in the constant movement of events. Far from it!

The idea of a resurrection of dead men was uncongenial to the minds of most of Paul's hearers. All of them but the Epicureans would no doubt have agreed with him had he spoken of the immortality of the individual soul; but as for resurrection, most of them would endorse the sentiments of the god Apollo, expressed when that very court of the Areopagus was founded by the city's patron goddess Athene: "Once a man dies and the earth drinks up his blood, there is *no resurrection*."[9]

Some observers of Paul's actions here suggest that perhaps he compromised the Christian position in his appeal to the intellectuals at Athens; they suggest he tried to use reason out of a proper framework to get them to understand and accept his message. They point to the scarcity of results and to the sneering reaction of many of the hearers. W. Graham Scroggie effectively answered this idea:

> Some think that this message was Paul's great failure: that he pandered to philosophy, and so failed. I do not accept that view. Did he fail? . . . Some mocked; some procrastinated; and some believed. . . . Is not that *always* the result of Gospel preaching? What is your attitude? Derision? delay? or decision?[10]

It appears from the total picture presented in Acts 17 that the proclamation of the gospel of Jesus had already been stated to the hearers at Athens. A close look at Acts 17:17 reveals that Paul was continuing his activity of reasoning in the synagogue and in the marketplace every day. Thus the activity of evangelism had been started. First, Paul stated the message of Jesus and, second, he offered a defense or response to their objections. In fact, these hearers had already heard the terms *resurrection* and *Jesus* in Paul's teaching. So in Acts 17, technically speaking, there is an expansion and clarification of the foundation of the gospel proclaimed by Paul.

Certainly there will never be another situation exactly like that which Paul faced. Yet in giving a defense with reference to philosophies that are foreign to Christian truth today, we can apply the principles followed by Paul. Several of these principles seem obvious. First, in building a point of contact between any philosophy of life and Christianity, the Christian defender should be an accurate observer and interpreter of the position that objects to Christianity. Notice that Paul astutely observed their practice and found a real point of contact in their acknowledged ignorance. True contact for defense does not imply compromise or a watering down of the Christian world and life view.

Second, in further clarifying Christian truth, Paul in Acts 17:28 quoted some non-Christian Greek writers. The apostle tacitly acknowledged that these statements, as far as they went, were an accurate assessment of the data in question—God's immanence and His providential control of life, as well as His creation of man. The lesson for any defender of Christian truth is obvious. We need to know the positions that we are seeking to answer, and we need to be alert to statements made within these positions that give opportunity to explain the truth of God. As N. B. Stonehouse noted:

> Paul could allow consistently and fully for the thought that pagan men, in spite of themselves and contrary to the controlling disposition of their minds, as creatures of God confronted with the divine revelation were capable of responses which were valid so long as and to the extent that they stood in isolation from their pagan systems. Thus, thoughts which in their pagan contexts were quite un-Christian and anti-Christian, could be acknowledged as up to a point involving an actual apprehension of revealed truth. As creatures of God, retaining a *sensus divinitatis* in spite of their sin, their ignorance of God and their suppression of the truth, they were not without a certain awareness of God and of their creaturehood.[11]

Therefore, Acts 17 certainly provides any student of apologetics with much material on which to reflect. It allows for sufficient real contact between the Christian and non-Christian positions. In giving a defense the Christian can follow the great principles enunciated by Paul and can be assured that God will vindicate His truth in His good pleasure.

CONCLUSION

All of these case studies have been approached with the basic understanding that they can supply possible patterns and guidelines. Yet we must avoid oversimplification and we must avoid attempting to think that there is only one correct way of giving a defense. The biblical patterns obviously allow different approaches to various questions. The Christian position is flexible enough and dynamic enough to provide a response to all false world views and philosophies. In contending earnestly for the faith (Jude 3), the

Christian defender must make a determined effort to function in the strength of the Holy Spirit, as Stephen did. Further, the Christian apologete must seek to make valid points of contact for Christian defense within the ideologies set against Christianity, as Paul did. Without compromise or a false appeal to man's pride, the Christian must give a cogent statement of defense that is in keeping with these biblical case studies.

REVIEW QUESTIONS

1. In Stephen's defense what was the statement of the case against Christianity?

2. Very concisely, how did he answer the charges of the case against Christianity?

3. What timeless principle can we draw from Stephen's example of apologetics?

4. Briefly, how does the truth of Galatians 3:10–13 show a Christian response to the charge of Judaism concerning the death of Jesus?

5. What lesson can we get from Paul's defense concerning the death of Jesus?

6. What point of contact did Paul establish with his hearers in Acts 17, and what was the real principle involved in this contact?

7. What place did Paul give to the resurrection of Jesus in his proclamation?

8. What evidence suggests that these hearers of Paul could not have taken the fact of the Resurrection and simply built it into their way of looking at reality?

9. How, specifically, do the fields of evangelism and apologetics relate in the data of Acts 17?

10. List and describe very briefly the principles that we can draw from Paul's statement on the Areopagus for apologetics.

FOR FURTHER READING

Bruce, F. F. *The Defense of the Gospel in the New Testament.* Rev. ed. Grand Rapids: Eerdmans, 1977. Pp. 14–49.

Schaeffer, Francis A. *2 Contents, 2 Realities.* Downers Grove, Ill.: InterVarsity, 1974. Pp. 15–20.

Stonehouse, Ned B. *The Areopagus Address.* London: Tyndale, 1949.

CHAPTER 4

New Testament Apologetics Continued: A Method of Defense

Paul wrote the Book of Colossians to help stabilize and strengthen some believers in their Christian life. The book provides another example of Christian defense. It reveals that in responding to false positions, a Christian apologete can be of great help also to fellow believers. In addition, Colossians shows that a bona fide by-product of strong defense is a strengthening of believers.

THE NON-CHRISTIAN CHALLENGE

The Epistle to the Colossians was written by the apostle Paul during his first Roman imprisonment. Many Christian scholars, following largely the pattern set by J. B. Lightfoot in his 1879 commentary entitled *Saint Paul's Epistles to the Colossians and Philemon*, have noted that Paul was obviously dealing with, among other issues, a problem that threatened the churches in the Lycus River valley even as early as the late 50s or early 60s A.D. With this background, Colossians can be studied as a step-by-step guide to Christian defense and confirmation.

It is apparent that a strange combination of ideas had found its way into the thinking and living of many non-Christians in that area. Because the believers needed to be strengthened and encouraged in the face of this teaching, Paul skillfully answered the false ideas as he presented the truth of Christ and His all-sufficiency.

While some doubt has been cast on the validity of Lightfoot's

47

interpretation of some of the teaching of Colossians, the major ideas he developed seem valid. Writing with much of the more recent scholarship at his disposal, F. F. Bruce concluded that

> at Colossae in particular there was a strong tendency among the Christians to embrace a form of teaching which (although they themselves had no suspicion of this) threatened to subvert the gospel of grace which they had recently believed and to replace their Christian liberty with spiritual bondage. To safeguard them against this threat Paul sent them the Epistle to the Colossians.[1]

The non-Christian system, if it might be thus designated, was a mixture of Jewish and Greek ideas, with a blending into this of some other ancient speculative elements. For the sake of convenience, some of the elements may be listed as follows:

RITUALISTIC ELEMENTS	SPECULATIVE ELEMENTS
ceremonialism (2:16)	Oriental mysticism;
observances;	an evil principle;
distinctions of food and drinks in asceticism (2:20–23)	worship of subordinate spirits (angels) (2:18)

THE CHRISTIAN RESPONSE

Colossians 2:8 reveals Paul's concern with reference to false teachings. "See to it that no one takes you captive through philosophy and empty deception, according the the tradition of men, according to the elementary principles of the world, rather than according to Christ." The urgency of Paul's warning is seen also when the first part of the verse is rendered as follows: "Be continually looking out that no one takes you captive through his philosophy." Perhaps Paul had learned about a certain leader whose teaching was popular in that area. The ideas presented might certainly have sounded intriguing to some of the believers. The ethnic background of the Colossians evidently played a part in this, for they were Phrygian Gentiles; and it is possible to trace their heritage back to roots that could tend to give them a highly emotional and mystical temperament. Tenney has summarized the entire situation well:

The heresy of Colosse which evoked this epistle was a local development which arose because of the peculiar situation of the city. Colosse was on the trade route from the East, along which oriental religions as well as oriental merchandise were transported to Rome. The Colossians were Phrygian Gentiles (1:27), whose religious antecedents were highly emotional and mystical. They were seeking to attain the fullness of God, and when teachers came among them with a philosophy that promised a mystic knowledge of God, they were entranced by it.[2]

The three major areas of confrontation that Paul chooses to deal with are the mind of man, the order of the universe, and the actual life of man. For each of these areas it will be sufficient to note the major non-Christian inference revealed by Paul's comments and then to list his major response.

The first consideration will be in the area of the mind. An appeal is made in the false teaching to a very exclusive and limited few to go on to higher learning, with the ultimate goal of perfection in view. The goal here was apparently to go on to a deeper and fuller knowledge by utilizing the mental powers inherent in the personality. It would seem that few could ultimately attain this. Paul's method was to deal with these ideas in a head-on confrontation. The apostle turned the attention of the Colossian believers to the truth that Christian maturity and the Christian life with its true goals are areas open to all individuals, not to just a few. His technique can be seen in Colossians 1:28, where key words are italicized: "And we proclaim Him, admonishing *every* man and teaching *every* man with all wisdom, that we may present *every* man complete in Christ." Certainly, the meaning of this verse is not exhausted by simply noting that its inclusive thrust seems to answer an exclusive elitism that some false teachers were stressing! But the fact remains that very possibly some of the total teaching content of this passage deals with a statement of truth intended to combat the false exclusivism.

Reverences to *wisdom, intelligence, knowledge,* and *perfect knowledge* are frequent in the book. Note the following: *wisdom* (Col. 1:9, 28; 2:3; 3:16; 4:5); *intelligence* (1:9; 2:2); *knowledge* (2:3); *perfect knowledge* (1:9–10; 2:2; 3:10). In response to a false knowledge and false pursuit of esoteric wisdom, Paul simply presents Christ as the source of all true wisdom and the worthwhile pattern for Christian maturity.

The second consideration moves in the area of the order of the universe. The false teaching probably included a stress on angels as being somehow involved in the ongoing process and order of the universe. The Greek term for their sphere of activity was *pleroma* (literally, "fullness"). In two major passages, Colossians 1:15–20 and 2:9–15, Paul unfolds the truth of Christ as being the Creator of all spheres and realms of creation, including angels. A very specific reference to the worship of angels appears in 2:18. The total teaching impact of this book is to reveal Christ as the Lord of all creation; and, indeed, He could be viewed as the "cosmic Christ."

The third consideration deals with the life of each individual person. Obvious references again to Christian personal ethics are found in Colossians 2:20–3:4. Paul warns his readers not to be taken in by a false teaching that stresses ritual observances. His positive teaching seems to be framed within a "no holds barred" response to some false ideas. He is not engaged in "shadow boxing." Rather, his concern is to teach these believers that Christ alone is the key to life in its fullest ethical dimension. Colossians 3:11 seems to mirror this fact. Christ is indeed all, and through Him the life of each believer is to be lived in real freedom from bondage to a false asceticism.

THE METHOD OF APOLOGETICS

The following summarizing principles emerge from studying Colossians. First, there is the principle of *contrast*. Paul's defense involved an exposure of the false ideas in the light of truth. In this sense Paul was really contrasting one system of thought, with its way of life, with the truth in Christ systematically unfolded.

Second, there is the principle of *comprehension*. Paul's masterful work in encouraging believers involves a deep and thorough knowledge and comprehension of the false system, right down to the very terms used and to the meanings and implications drawn.

Third, there is the principle of *clarification*. A true Christian defense involves a positive clarification and explanation of Christian truth. This is patently clear from the positive teaching unfolded in Colossians.

Fourth, there is the principle of *confirmation*. Christian apologetics can involve the encouragement and confirmation of believers in the truth. Often, a study of Christian apologetics and evidences can be of help in strengthening believers and pointing them to the deep verities of their relationship to God as based squarely on truth and not on falsehood.

Bruce has written a succinct summary of this entire matter as it relates to a study of apologetics:

> In his defence of the gospel against this plausible system, Paul gives a good example of his readiness to be "all things to all men" for the gospel's sake (I Cor. 9:22f.). He confronts the false *gnōsis* and bodily asceticism which was being urged upon the Colossian Christians with the true *gnōsis* and spiritual asceticism of Christ. While he writes as an uncompromising opponent of the false teaching, he takes up its characteristic terms and shows how the truth which they attempt, unsuccessfully, to convey is embodied in Christ, the true "mystery" (or revelation) of God.
>
> In this Epistle, it has been argued, Paul is undertaking two tasks at once—the defence of Christianity over against the intellectual world of paganism and the defence of gospel truth within the church. As an apologist to the Gentiles, he was perhaps the first to meet his pagan opponents on their own ground, and use their language in a Christian sense to make it clear that the problems to which they vainly sought an answer elsewhere found their satisfying solution in Christ.[3]

In constructing a method for contemporary apologetics, we must certainly take these principles into consideration in our serious attempts to respond to false systems. In the light of modern scientific advances and the opening up of space technology, it would appear that the stabilizing and strengthening power of the same cosmic Lord Jesus Christ that Paul experienced and to which he directed his Colossian readers can and still does enable Christians today to respond to false systems and to live meaningfully.

REVIEW QUESTIONS

1. Outline briefly the elements of the non-Christian teaching that may have been influencing the people of Colosse.

2. What appeal in the area of the mind of man did this false system make, and how did Paul respond to it?

3. How did the false teaching stress angels, and what did Paul say about this?

4. List and explain briefly each of the principles that emerge from Paul's statement of defense in Colossians.

FOR FURTHER READING

Bruce, F. F. *The Defense of the Gospel in the New Testament.* Rev. ed. Grand Rapids: Eerdmans, 1977. Chap. 6, pp. 70–88.

Lightfoot, J. B. *Commentary on St. Paul's Epistles to the Colossians and Philemon.* Classic Commentary Library. Grand Rapids: Zondervan, 1957. Pp. 73–113.

Thomas, W. H. Griffith. *Outline Studies in the Acts of the Apostles.* Edited by Winifred T. Gillespie. Grand Rapids: Eerdmans, 1956. Pp. 343–60.

CHAPTER 5

Faith and Reason
in Apologetics

Some valuable lessons can be gained by considering a few methods of building a defense of Christianity against non-Christian systems of thought. The specific issue here turns on the question of what shall be the ultimate ground of appeal in developing a basic defense. Will the apologetic rest on faith alone for final vindication? Will it rest on reason predominantly, even to the deemphasis of faith, as a ground of response to the non-Christian objector's challenges? Or, will it rest on a balance of faith and reason? Various combinations of the elements of faith and reason have been suggested by apologetes, and it is now necessary that we examine the options carefully.

BASIC DEFINITIONS

For the sake of this discussion, *faith* will be described as meaningful confidence or belief in the truthfulness of the Christian position, and the term will be viewed as practically synonymous with trust. A helpful comparison of terms in a nontechnical sense has been given as follows:

> *Trust, faith, confidence* . . . these nouns refer to a feeling that a person or thing will not fail in performance. *Trust* implies depth and assurance of such feeling. . . . When acceptance of someone or something is unquestioning and emotionally charged, *faith* is the more appropriate term. Confidence suggests less intensity of feeling but, frequently, good evidence for being sure.[1]

The term *reason* will be described as a process of sound or straight thinking that moves in the realm of the process of logical analysis. Often the term implies all the activity of reasoning, which can be described as "the mental processes of one who reasons; especially, the drawing of conclusions or inferences from observations, facts, or hypotheses. . . the evidence or arguments used in this procedure."[2]

THE PRIORITY OF REASON IN APOLOGETICS

A Proponent of This View

Ramon Lull (c. 1232–1316) was an example of a spokesman for Christianity who believed that predominantly by a process of thinking and reasoning the objections raised against Christianity could be silenced. Lull, or Lully, as his name sometimes appears, was a Roman Catholic who was converted to Christianity in adulthood, and whose purpose was to win Muslims to Christianity. During missionary journeys to Islamic-dominated Tunis and Algeria, he practiced his method of argumentation and apologetics. A noted philosopher described Lull as a man

> who dedicates himself, with a slightly chimerical ardor, to the propagation of a homemade method of apologetics which will infallibly bring about the conversion of unbelievers.
>
> Lull's famous *Art* is the exposition of that method. It consists essentially in circles on which are inscribed the fundamental concepts, in such a way that by combining the various possible positions of these circles with regard to one another, one can automatically obtain all the relations of concepts corresponding to the essential verities of religion. It must be confessed that when we today try to use those tables, we come up against the worst difficulties, and one cannot help wondering whether Lull himself was ever able to use them. If we confine ourselves to his own declaration, we must believe he was, the more so as we could not otherwise conceive the insistence with which he advocated the use of his *Art* against the errors of the Averroists and the Moslems.[3]

The Basic Position

As seen in the preceding quotation, Lull believed that reason was supreme in the matter of conquering opposition to Christianity. His complicated tables and drawings comprising his *Great Art (Ars*

Magna) are now viewed by most mathematicians and students of logic as irrelevant. However, the purpose of the work that Lull engaged in must not be overlooked. He insisted that God had given him by direct vision the substance of this work and he constantly emphasized that such apologetic activity as answering the objections raised by Moslems by the use of geometrical designs was indispensable as a tool for bringing about the conversion of these unbelievers. Lest one think that this unusual and even eccentric position has gone overlooked in the scholarly community, it should be noted that in the book entitled *Logic Machines and Diagrams* by Martin Gardner (New York: McGraw-Hill, 1958), the entire first chapter is devoted to a critical analysis of this fascinating subject of Lull's work. The chapter is filled with pictures of Lull's complex circles and geometrical designs. These devices were something like a circular slide rule that was useful in science classes prior to the age of the hand-held calculator! Gardner noted:

> Lull had managed to finish writing . . . his first book, the *Book of Contemplation*. It is a massive, dull work of several thousand pages that seeks to prove by "necessary reason" all the major truths of Christianity. Thomas Aquinas had previously drawn a careful distinction between truths of natural theology that he believed could be established by reason, and truths of revelation that could be known only by faith. Lull found this distinction unnecessary. He believed that all the leading dogmas of Christianity, including the trinity and incarnation, could be demonstrated by irrefutable arguments, although there is evidence that he regarded "faith" as a valuable aid in understanding such proofs.[4]

Whatever one might think about Lull, it is certain that he represented, in an extreme manner to be sure, the concept held by some that the process of thinking known as reasoning will achieve the ultimate answer to all non-Christian thought. Furthermore, Lull thought reason could impell acquiescence on the part of objectors concerning the truthfulness of Christianity.

The Problem With the View

One senses immediately the imbalance in this view that makes reasoning as a process of thinking predominant in the ultimate vindication of Christian truth. Lull failed to distinguish between apologetics and evangelism. Furthermore, there is a failure in this view to recognize the difference between the acknowledgment of truth and the acceptance of truth. This position seems to imply that the process of thinking would create faith and would move the will of the objector. In Lull's way of looking at it, if he could convince the objector intellectually by his process of reasoning, there would be an automatic shift on the part of the objector from acknowledgment of truth to acceptance of truth. Deeper analysis of all the biblical issues here can easily convince us that acceptance of truth involves the decision of the entire person, and this includes the function of the will, the intellect, and the emotions. Bernard Ramm succinctly summarized the real problem with Lull's position, or with any position that gives a disproportionate place to the process of reasoning alone without the balance of faith:

> There is an exaggeration of the intellectual in man. Lully's proposition is that truth is to be grasped by rationalized intellect. This would convert us all into logicians if we really wanted to know the truth. But neither life, nor experience, nor nature is this highly intellectualized. In a small or larger degree, intuition, insight, emotion, and aesthetics all go into human consciousness in its quest for truth.[5]

Certainly, there is a grave danger in oversimplifying things here. It does appear that in Lull's work reason has taken on the dimension of a construction of inferences drawn from mathematic-like tables or charts. Reason correctly defined includes where feasible a process of analysis, but it assuredly includes far more than what Lull did in constructing his circles and drawings. Nonetheless, there is the implication here that a process of mental activity will make it possible for the acceptance of Christian truth to come automatically by the intellect alone. As is often the case, there is some truth in a position that also manifests imbalance. The part is not the whole, and thus we turn elsewhere for a pathway of defense that can bring into balance faith and reason.

THE PRIORITY OF FAITH IN APOLOGETICS

A Proponent of This View

Sören Kierkegaard (1813–1855), a Danish philosopher, could feasibly be listed as an advocate of the view that faith should be given priority in apologetics. In giving a defense or statement of Christianity, Kierkegaard could exemplify the idea or concept of faith as the major factor in the vindication of Christianity. This predominance would be seen as over against reason, or a process of examining the evidence for the truth claims of Christianity. Again, there is no attempt made here to deal exhaustively with the nuances of Kierkegaardian existentialism, or to assign this title to any and all who would elevate faith to the extent of imbalance.

The Position Stated

In striking contrast to the position of Ramon Lull, that of Kierkegaard could be said to begin with the acceptance of almost a complete skepticism concerning a person's innate ability to know anything. In fact, the real answer to a person's ultimate need must come with the starting point of recognizing absolute hopelessness, even despair, in the realm of mental activity for learning truth about God. The development of this sense of despair drove Kierkegaard to the position that there is no evidence that can function in the realm of objective data that would reveal the truth about God. Thus in defending his interpretation of Christianity against objectors, Kierkegaard did not appeal to any process of reasoning whatever concerning the claims of Christ, the ground of theistic belief, or any of the more traditional apologetic activities. Instead, he appealed to a leap of faith, as it were, a blind, irrational casting of oneself on some agent or being called "God"; thereby he experienced in this encounter of faith the momentary enlightenment of knowledge and certitude. In discussing how this encounter occurs, Kierkegaard said:

> But in relation to Christianity he believes against the understanding and in this case also uses understanding . . . to make sure that he believes against the understanding . . . but he makes so much use of the understanding that he becomes aware of the incomprehensible, and then he holds to this, believing against the understanding.[6]

This was a must unusual way of describing faith. Yet there is an attitude on the part of many individuals, regardless of their knowledge or lack of it concerning Kierkegaard, that seems to imply this bifurcation of faith and reason or thinking. The implication here for apologetics is critical, of course. The best defense here would seem to include holding out only a description of the supposed leap of faith and not to develop propositions showing the reasonableness of faith. Also, the best defense would include establishing skepticism about human knowledge, then answering all objections with an appeal to radical commitment to Christ.

The Position Analyzed

A concise analysis of this position reveals significant problems. A major difficulty is the incomplete view of faith that Sören Kierkegaard espoused. In this view faith becomes far less than the full-orbed biblical trust or confidence in the person and work of the Lord Jesus Christ. Classical descriptions of the activity of saving faith formally identify these elements: an intellectual element, or activity of thought *(notitia)*; an emotional element, or activity of feeling *(assensus)*; a volitional element, or activity of trust *(fiducia)*. A. H. Strong perceptively illustrated these three strands of truth as follows:

> The three constituents of faith may be illustrated from the thought, feeling, and action of a person who stands by a boat, upon a little island which the rising stream threatens to submerge. He first regards the boat from a purely intellectual point of view—it is merely an *actually existing boat*. As the stream rises, he looks at it, secondly, with some accession of emotion—his prospective danger awakens in him the conviction that it is a *good boat for a time of need*, though he is not yet ready to make use of it. But, thirdly, when he feels that the rushing tide must otherwise sweep him away, a volitional element is added—he gets into the boat, trusts himself to it, accepts it as his *present, and only, means of safety*. Only this last faith in the boat is faith that saves, although this last includes both the preceding. It is equally clear that the getting into the boat may actually save a man, while at the same time he may be full of fears that the boat will never bring him to shore. These fears may be removed by the boatman's word.[7]

In Kierkegaard's view the intellectual element of faith is neglected, even forsaken. Edward J. Carnell (1919–1967), apologete and theologian, pointed out with devastating accuracy the massive problem of Kierkegaard and any one else who would sever faith from objectivity. He stated:

When the supreme value is brought into the discussion, namely, faith in God, the heart can think of absolutely no reason why the axiom which guides us in all other axiological situations should now suddenly fail. If God's existence is of infinite concern to us, we ought to express infinite determination to obey, rather than defy, the understanding. Since the gods of the heathen, like the poor, are with us always, it behooves a rational man to be exceedingly cautious when he worships deity. In his enthusiasm to find Christ he might wind up worshiping non-Christ, and so lose all through his rational mismanagement. Does one adorn his faith to say, "My understanding assures me that the historical Jesus is the revelation of God's *agape* in the flesh; but since I experience less passion if I respect objective evidences, I passionately believe that God has revealed himself through a motley land turtle"?[8]

This point is so crucial to the issue of defense of the faith that it must be emphasized with real force. In giving defense, the ultimate ground of appeal will move primarily in the realm of response to intellectual objections raised. To be sure, however, the Christian defender knows also that the person who brings objections is made up of a complex interrelationship of intellect, sensibility, and will. In the final and ultimate decision of the will, we know that God the Holy Spirit is the agent in the massive work of regeneration (Titus 3:5). Yet it is certain that saving faith is grounded on solid truth and fact. The method of giving defense will not redefine faith, as Kierkegaard did, but will function within the balanced view of faith presented in the classic interrelationship of thought, feeling, and trust. Francis A. Schaeffer's interesting narrative on the concluding pages of his book *He Is There and He Is Not Silent* fittingly summarizes the meaning of true faith and the place of argumentation in apologetics with a story about mountain climbers in the Alps. The climbers are suddenly fogged in as they are scaling bare rock. The guide directs the group to keep climbing. Finally, one of the climbers asks the guide about simply dropping down in order to come to rest on a supposed ledge ten feet below (unseen) and thus find some safe place until the fog would lift. The guide would say that this might be a possibility. So, with no knowledge or any reason to back up this action, one of the climbers "hangs and drops into the fog. This would be one kind of faith, a leap of faith."[9]

Now, as the story unfolds, suppose that the climbers hear a voice ring out in the midst of that arduous activity as the fog settles in and ice continues to form on the rock. The speaker announces that he is a veteran mountaineer who knows every foot of that area; he assures the group that even though they cannot see it, there is a safety spot just below them. He advises that they should go ahead and take the action of faith, that is, drop down on the unseen ledge. Now, Schaeffer says, a person in that group would not just implicitly do what that voice advised. He would ask questions, even in his predicament of danger, not out of idle curiosity, but because of the seriousness of the situation. For example, he would want to know the speaker's identity and if he really knew that region. One clue would be to ask his name. If it matched the kind of names prevalent in that area, this would be some indication that the speaker was telling the truth. Schaeffer concludes:

> For example, in the area of the Alps where I live, Avanthey would be such a name. In my desperate situation, even though time would be running out, *I would ask him what to me would be the sufficient questions,* and when I became convinced by his answers, then I would hang and drop.
>
> This is faith, but obviously it has no relationship to the first instance. As a matter of fact, if one of these is called faith, the other should not be designated by the same word symbol. The historic Christian faith is not a leap of faith in the post-Kierkegaardian sense because "he is not silent," and *I am invited to ask the sufficient questions in regard to details but also in regard to the existence of the universe and its complexity and in regard to the existence of man. I am invited to ask the sufficient questions* and then believe him and bow before him metaphysically in knowing that I exist because he made man, and bow before him morally as needing his provision for me in the substitutionary, propitiatory death of Christ.[10] (italics mine)

The work of apologetics in this narrative is that activity of answering the sufficient questions in regard to the details of the authoritative voice of the veteran mountaineer. Possibly the analogy intended by Schaeffer here would be that the authentic voice of the God of creation has spoken definitively and with finality in the Word of God, Scripture, and in the person of the incarnate Deity, the God-man, the Lord Jesus Christ. Apologetics appeals to the understanding and the thinking process of the questioner in answering the questions. The final acceptance of the truth does not violate the acknowledgment of the truth in the mind. This shows the place of apologetics in "preevangelism" and yet also shows that the step of faith and of commitment must involve the total person and the commitment of the intellect, sensibility, and will. If one carried the narrative on to a logical conclusion, it would be possible to describe the terrified questioner, hanging there on the rock precipice, as hearing the answers and evaluating the evidence of the truthfulness of the mountaineer, but still rejecting that evidence and perishing. This is exactly the tragic situation of reality for those who do not transfer trust over to Christ as Mediator. In keeping within the original framework of the discussion, Kierkegaard would most likely have said that the person hanging on the rock precipice in obvious danger could not possibly ask the right kind of questions. In fact, that person would increase his or her danger by asking questions and would be better off if no voice whatever had spoken. In the Kierkegaardian and existentialist framework, the voice would be heard *after* the leap of faith; and it would be heard in an inward or subjective feeling of assurance, not as an objective and objectively verifiable voice. Thus we must look elsewhere than to Kierkegaard for the balance of faith and reason in giving a defense.

THE BALANCE OF FAITH AND REASON IN APOLOGETICS

A Proponent of This Position

Benjamin B. Warfield (1851–1921), American Presbyterian theologian who taught theology at Princeton Theological Seminary from 1887 to 1921, was a Christian leader who emphasized a balance of faith and reason in giving a defense. The position he espoused preserved the positive strengths of the two preceding views and avoided the imbalances of each of them. Warfield's penetrating analysis of the issues here speaks with timely relevance even to the present situation in the matter of apologetics and apologetic systems.

The Position Stated

Warfield was determined to show that the Christian faith is grounded on truth and on fact. He noted that while sin certainly radically affected all the faculties of man as far as man's ability to *believe* and *obey* the truth goes, it did not affect man's ability to *understand* the reasons for the truth. According to Warfield, sin did not affect a person's ability to understand arguments given in response to objections to the truth (or in response to the questions asked by the terrified mountain climber in Schaeffer's illustration). Warfield explained that both believers and unbelievers have the same abilities of thinking (he called this quality of thought *intellection*). Sin has affected every person, and apart from God's gracious action no one will believe and obey the truth. But Warfield cogently noted that if we drive a wedge between the process of thinking involved in hearing evidence for the truth of Christianity and the process of thinking involved in responding to that truth, we have ultimately severed Christian truth from its foundation in factuality.

To put Warfield's view into perspective, we must first note his concept of the thinking or reasoning process of the unbeliever who is asking the sufficient questions, as Schaeffer proposed. Warfield stated:

> Sin has not destroyed or altered in its essential nature any one of man's faculties, although—since it corrupts *homo totus*—it has affected the operation of them all. The depraved man neither thinks, nor feels, nor wills as he ought.[11]

Again, this point is vitally important for apologetics. The case study of the Olsens referred to earlier vindicates Warfield's view with telling force. The searching and questioning mind of the unregenerate person can perceive the answers given from the ground of apologetics. Christians should not postulate two different kinds of knowing or epistemologies, one for the knowing of truths of faith and the other for the knowing of truths of history. The balanced view of faith takes note of the concepts that *perception* of truth can lead to *reception* of truth and that the truth received and the truth perceived will be identical. To explain the proper balance of faith and reason, Warfield noted:

> It is equally easy to say that Christianity is attained, not by demonstrations, but by a new birth. Nothing could be more true. But neither could anything be more unjustified than the inferences that are drawn from this truth for the discrediting of Apologetics. It certainly is

not in the power of all the demonstrations in the world to make a Christian. Paul may plant and Apollos water; it is God alone who gives the increase. But it does not seem to follow that Paul would as well, therefore, not plant, and Apollos as well not water. . . . it does not in the least follow that the faith that God gives is an irrational faith, that is, a faith without grounds in right reason. . . . The Holy Spirit does not work a blind, an ungrounded faith in the heart. . . . We believe in Christ because it is rational to believe in him, not though it be irrational. . . .

We are not absurdly arguing that Apologetics has in itself the power to make a man a Christian or to conquer the world to Christ. Only the Spirit of Life can communicate life to a dead soul, or can convict the world in respect of sin, and of righteousness, and of judgment. But we are arguing that faith is, in all its exercises alike, a form of conviction, and is therefore, necessarily grounded in evidence.[12]

Such were the ingredients that Warfield included as he explained how faith and reason may be properly related and integrated. In contradistinction to the view represented by Ramon Lull, this more balanced position clearly states that all the elements of faith must be seen. According to Warfield, the will must be energized by God's Spirit in the finalized step of commitment and trust in the "faith complex" of intellect, sensibility, and will. Thus Warfield used reason in the balanced manner of its proper framework, and he showed that it is only a part of the total vindication process, not the whole process. In contrast to the view represented by Kierkegaard, this position carefully notes that God the Holy Spirit does indeed bear witness to propositional truth and that this truth is verifiable and open to investigation. The process of thinking engaged in by non-Christian objectors to the faith can be met with argumentation moving along the same kind of patterns that gave rise to the objections. The questions can be answered. The answers, in the scope of apologetics, do not energize the will to obedience of the truth, but they most assuredly are correct, grounded in ultimate truth, and satisfactory in the verification process. In the Schaeffer illustration cited earlier, the answers given from Christianity to the questions raised by the searcher reveal the fact that the authoritative Word of God has been given concerning the human predicament. The reasons for the faith once for all delivered to the saints are indeed verifiable and trustworthy. On such a basis as this, apologetics can function properly and within the prescribed sphere of its job description.

REVIEW QUESTIONS

1. How can the term *faith* be described as it is used in this chapter?
2. By comparison, how is the term *reason* used?
3. Briefly describe the position that Ramon Lull advocated.
4. Specifically, what did Lull believe that the process of thinking or reasoning would achieve in relationship to the non-Christian?
5. What is the problem with this view of reason?
6. Describe concisely the position called "priority of faith" in apologetics. Who propounded this position?
7. According to this view, what would be the best defense for Christianity?
8. State the three elements of faith and note specifically which element in Kierkegaard's view is neglected.
9. In the narrative used by Francis A. Schaeffer, what exactly is the activity of apologetics?
10. Compare briefly Warfield's view with that of Kirkegaard concerning the activity of apologetics.
11. Compare Warfield's view with that of Lull.

FOR FURTHER READING

Geisler, Norman L. and Feinberg, Paul D. "The Relationship Between Faith and Reason." Chap. 17 in *Introduction to Philosophy: A Christian Perspective*. Grand Rapids: Baker, 1980.

Miller, Ed L. *Classical Statements on Faith and Reason*. New York: Random, 1970.

Ramm, Bernard. "Lecture I: Faith and Reason." In *Problems in Christian Apologetics*. Portland, Ore.: Western Baptist Theological Seminary, 1949.

Warfield, Benjamin B. "Introductory Note." The article referred to in this chapter appears in various collections of Warfield material. It appears, for example, in Volume 2 of the collection edited by John E. Meeter and entitled *Selected Shorter Writings of Benjamin B. Warfield*. Nutley, N.J.: Presbyterian and Reformed, 1970.

CHAPTER 6

Apologetics, Common Ground, and Related Scripture Passages

In studying apologetics the Christian soon confronts the question of common ground. It involves very specifically this question: Just how much of our defense and our argumentation can we expect the objectors to understand and assimilate when we realize that they need to trust the Redeemer as their personal Savior in order to enter into the realm of Christian life and truth? If there can be really no common ground between the Christian and the objector, why even bother to speak back and to articulate the Christian faith and its answers? What possible good can come from this activity?

THE QUESTION OF COMMON GROUND

Common Ground Described

The term *common ground* has been used to designate the common range of understanding that a Christian and a non-Christian have about truth and life. In this sense the expression refers to a common usage of terms by persons of different beliefs. The use of common terms is seen in the Congress of the United States. In the Senate, for example, when action is conducted on the floor, there are terms, meanings, and functions that are similar and that hold true for any senator, whether he or she is a Democrat or a Republican. Thus each senator functions within a framework of meaning. Terms such as "to make a motion" and "to second a motion" mean the same thing to all senators regardless of their party affiliation. Having defined and illustrated common ground, let us now look at the term in more detail, with special emphasis on its vital relationship to the methods of apologetics.

Common Ground Delineated

The level of communication. At the level of the communication of ideas and the use of speech and thinking processes, there is common ground—agreement between the Christian defender and the non-Christian objector who needs to hear a response. This is the level of language and of real contact where person-to-person confrontation occurs. Great care must be exercised in analyzing this area of common ground. Some serious defenders of the faith feel they are compromising the Christian position if they grant *any* common ground to the non-Christian objector. They feel that the position of Christian truth is sacrificed if, for example, both the believer and the unbeliever are seen to have the same process of thinking and to function within the use of reasoning as a tool. The process of reasoning and logical analysis is sometimes called "Aristotelian logic." Somehow this seems to imply that thinking processes or logical analysis will function at two different levels, the Christian and the non-Christian.

One modern defender of Christian truth shows how incongruous it is to think that a non-Christian and a Christian have no common ground in the matter of thinking, or process of intellection, as Warfield called it. While not directed exactly to this issue originally, the statement that follows nevertheless has a real bearing on the question of common ground:

> "Aristotelian logic" is a catch phrase. . . . It implies wrongly that Aristotle's basic laws of logic are just one option among many. The truth is that all forms of logic or thought (deductive, inductive, symbolic, or whatever) must use the law of noncontradiction. Further, the phrase "Aristotelian logic" often implies that Aristotle invented it. He did not; at best, he was the first in the west to write systematically about it. God is the ontological basis for logic. It is based on his self-consistent and rational thoughts.[1]

Applying this decisive statement to the matter of common ground, we find that objections are raised against the Christian faith and articulated in words. Words move in patterns of meanings and are tools to express thoughts. These words express the thoughts of individuals. It goes without saying that the person doing this *understands* what is being said in articulating an objection to Christian truth. Reduced to its simplest dimension, the conclusion to be drawn from the fact of common ground is this: If the critic, who needs to be answered (Titus 1:9), can articulate and understand the objection that is raised, then he or she can understand the answer given by the Christian apologete. If we deny this, we seem to implicate ourselves in a rather tenuous position. We seem to say that there is one process of articulating and thinking and expressing thoughts that the non-Christian follows and another that the Christian follows, and that the two never meet. The problem with this is that the ground of data common to both includes a process of thinking (the use of the law of contradiction, for example), thinking about evidence for Christian truth and thinking about evidence raised against Christian truth. If we really believe that there is no common ground at this level, we defeat the entire purpose of apologetics, and thereby our "mouths are stopped," rather than "stopping the mouths" of the opposition (cf. Titus 1:11 KJV).

Furthermore, the very gospel of Jesus Christ is communicated through words, language, and meaning. This very gospel rests on great historical facts (1 Cor. 15:1–3). These facts are enunciated, stated, and interpreted in words. If we make these great Christian words (*atonement, redemption, reconciliation,* and so forth) subject to a distinctive pattern of thinking and reasoning, a so-called "spiritual" level of thinking that transcends the normal level of thought and process of thinking, we effectively destroy the very ground of the Christian faith, perhaps innocently, and even in the name of Christian truth!

The level of classification. At the level of the classification of ideas and interpretation of data, there is still common ground between the Christian and the non-Christian. For example, in a study of science both the Christian botanist and the non-Christian botanist agree, for the sake of classification, on a battery of terms and their definitions. Now, to be sure, the issue of common ground at this point becomes somewhat complicated. Thus in referring to the so-called "taxonomic tree of life," the Christian botanist or zoologist uses the terms and classification nomenclature that the non-Christian does. Yet all the while the Christian *knows* and *understands* from the ground of truth revealed in sacred Scripture that a personal God is the source of all creation. The believer in this situation knows that the terms of classification are tools only and that these terms must function within a total "model," a pattern or scheme of interpretation. At this point there is a sharper distinction, particularly in the realm of science, over interpreting data that are common to both the Christian and non-Christian. If we stated that there is unqualified common ground at the level of communication, we would have to say that there is qualified common ground at the level of classification. In some cases there will be sharp differentiation and even separation between the Christian and non-Christian at this level of contact.

The level of correlation. There is no common ground postulated between the Christian and the non-Christian when they move into the level of correlating all knowledge into a coherent system, the ultimate level of a total view of all reality. For example, the Christian who understands something of the wonderful works of the God of creation in the study of science cannot ultimately have common ground with the non-Christian who rejects the truth of God and who attempts to spin out an entire philosophy that leaves God out of the position.

Summary. Person to person, there is real common ground existing with reference to the Christian and the non-Christian. Term for term, as far as science is concerned, there still exists some common ground. System for system, as far as ultimate meaning goes, there is no common ground existing between the adherent of the Christian world and life view and the adherent of any competing systematic attempt to correlate all reality without the knowledge of God. To be sure, these levels are interrelated, and any differentiation scheme like the one just presented is open to the danger of oversimplification. However, the entire craft of apologetics, of giving defense, functions within the assumed position that in contending earnestly for the faith, the Christian can actually speak answers *into* a context *out of which* objections have come. This speaking involves communication, an appeal to a process of thinking that must characterize all human beings.

RELATED SCRIPTURE PASSAGES

There are some passages of Scripture that have a vital bearing on common ground and indeed on the entire realm of the activity of apologetics.

1 Corinthians 1:17–31

Arguments against false systems and careful reasoning seem strangely out of place when one considers the strong words recorded in this passage. Paul explains cogently that the preaching of the gospel is "not with wisdom of words" (v. 17 KJV). In fact, he goes on to note that it appears to be folly or foolishness to those who reject it and are perishing (v. 18). If this be the case, one might well ask: What about all the arguments involved in apologetics? Are they not mere "wisdom of words"? If so, how can God be glorified in that kind of activity?

A solid guide to interpreting any portion of Scripture is to allow the context of the passage or Scripture segment to control the consideration. This context is describing the proclamation of the gospel of Christ, not the articulation of a reason for the Christian hope. It is transparently clear that Paul is describing the presentation of the Christian message with reference to the problems faced by the church at Corinth. That church was plagued with divisions, and these divisions were built around a factious spirit that involved honoring one human leader above another (1 Cor. 1:11–13). Coupled with this fact was the background truth that these Greeks loved to hear skilled oratory. One commentator notes:

> Some at least of the Corinthians were setting too high a value on human wisdom and human eloquence in line with the typical Greek admiration for rhetoric and philosophical studies. In the face of this Paul insists that preaching *with wisdom of words* was no part of his commission. That kind of preaching would draw men to the preacher. It would nullify the cross of Christ. The faithful preaching of the cross results in men ceasing to put their trust in any human device, and relying rather on God's work in Christ. A reliance on rhetoric would cause men to trust in men, the very antithesis of what the preaching of the cross is meant to effect.[2]

The words of this great passage of Scripture do not place a restriction on activity that would simply seek to answer charges brought against Christian truth. Far from it! The passage indicates that there is a legitimate source for all wisdom, namely, "Christ the power of God and the wisdom of God" (1 Cor. 1:24). Seen in the light of its context, this passage was not written to place restrictions on apologetics, but to show the believers at Corinth that they had to keep before their thinking constantly the radical truth that their lives must be built squarely on the wisdom of God and not on the wisdom of people or on the eloquent speech of people. There is no problem here, therefore, with reference to the practice of apologetics.

1 Corinthians 2:10–14

Here is another passage of Scripture that unfolds the graphic portrait of the inability of people to comprehend spiritual things apart from spiritual insight. Accurate conclusions must be drawn from these verses and a determined effort made to interpret and apply them accurately.

Verse 11 states, "For who among men knows the *thoughts* of a man except the spirit of the man, which is in him? Even so the *thoughts* of God no one knows except the Spirit of God." The primary teaching of this passage clearly speaks of the need for the illuminating work of the Holy Spirit in the entire area of the reception of spiritual truth and the interpretation of truth. The word *knows* in the second part of verse 11 is the Greek word *ginōskō*. The Greek words for *knowing* and *knowledge* form a rich ground for interpretive study. *Ginōskō* in its pattern of usage implies the knowledge of deep personal understanding, and often denotes experiential knowledge, realization, and appropriation. Another Greek word for knowing, *oida*, moves more often to denote intellectual apprehension and knowledge of a more objective and less experiential nature.[3]

The primary teaching of verse 11, based on the actual words used, seems clearly to be this: Only the Spirit of God knows in the depth of experiential knowledge the deep things of God. This is assuredly true, for the Spirit shares totally the essential being and nature of God since the Spirit indeed is God. Paul lays this foundation to build solid teaching concerning the need for the Spirit of God to enlighten believers concerning spiritual truth. His point seems to be this: If the Spirit of God is the only one who really knows the things of God, then the believer needs to depend on the Spirit and draw on His gracious work in understanding spiritual truth.

Verse 11 most assuredly *does not* forbid responding to an attack brought against Christian truth! Rather, this verse *does* assert that the things, truths, or deep purposes of God are known experientially and vitally only by the Spirit of God. Verse 12 goes on to indicate that this same Spirit has been received by every believer, and this opens up an avenue for the believer to have access to knowledge of the deeper truths involved in God's purpose and plan. Throughout this entire context, there is absolutely no reference to involvement with positions that oppose the Christian faith.

The statements in 1 Corinthians 2:14 seem to be describing the non-Christian response to Christian truth: "But a natural man does not accept the things of the Spirit of God; for they are foolishness to him, and he cannot understand them, because they are spiritually appraised." This verse categorically states that "the things of the Spirit of God" are not "accept[ed]" (received) by the "natural man" (the non-Christian). Now this does seem to get right into the issue of the non-Christian's objections to Christian truth.

It is imperative first to define what is meant by "the things of the Spirit of God" (v. 14a). A close study of the context, starting with verse 10, seems to suggest that these "things" are related to "the depths of God" (v. 10); "the *thoughts* of God" (v. 11); "the things freely given to us by God" (v. 12); and "which things we also speak, not in words taught by human wisdom, but in those taught by the Spirit" (v. 13). It seems that this includes the deep truths of our salvation in Christ, God's gracious indwelling through His Holy Spirit, and the entire program of God's grace. Most assuredly, this spiritual insight is a completely gracious provision of God that is totally foreign to the thinking of the non-Christian world.

Thus the key to understanding this passage lies in a careful appraisal of the words and the context. Verse 14 teaches that the non-Christian "does not accept the things of the Spirit of God"; furthermore, it teaches that "he cannot understand them." The Greek word for "understand" in verse 14 is *ginōskō*, implying deep, personal, and appropriating knowledge. A knowledge of the first part of verse 14 is crucial to seeing what the entire passage says: "But a natural man does not accept the things of the Spirit of God." The phrase "does not accept" is a translation of the Greek words *ou deketai*. This phrase *does not mean* "'is incapable of receiving,' but 'does not accept,' *i.e.*, he rejects, refuses."[4] The matter of *perception* is one thing, but the matter of *reception* is something entirely different. In its entirety verse 14 teaches that the unsaved person cannot experientially know the things of the Spirit of God. It furthermore shows that an unsaved person's refusal to obey the truth is based on rejection of the Christian position, at least to some degree, and not on incapacity to perceive it.

By preserving the distinction made between evangelism and apologetics, we keep a helpful perspective in interpreting 1 Corinthians 2:14. In regard to evangelism—the presentation of the truth of the gospel and all that the gospel involves—the unsaved person needs to experience the miraculous working of the Holy Spirit in opening the heart, even as Lydia did (Acts 16:14). In regard to apologetics and responding to challenges brought by the non-Christian against the Christian faith, the very challenge that is brought virtually demands an answer. First Corinthians 2:14 does not state that the non-Christian is incapable of perceiving an answer, but rather that he or she will not receive the truth. Again, the entire passage is explaining the deep truth involved in the illuminating work of the Holy Spirit in making spiritual truth known to believers. There is no ground for concluding from this passage that non-Christians cannot perceive answers given to them in response to objections raised. Furthermore, this passage most assuredly does not mean that Christians should close their mouths and not respond to objections brought against the truth!

2 Corinthians 4:3–4

This passage strikingly portrays the desperate need of people for enlightenment from the Holy Spirit if they are ever to receive the gospel. It might appear from a superficial reading of this passage that it would eliminate any need for a response to objections brought against the Christian faith, that is, any need for apologetics. The text states, "And even if our gospel is veiled, it is veiled to those who are perishing, in whose case the god of this world has blinded the minds of the unbelieving, that they might not see the light of the gospel of the glory of Christ, who is the image of God." The context and wording of the passage clearly set forth the seriousness of the gospel. The issue here is the gospel itself, that is, evangelism, and not apologetics. R. V. G. Tasker sets the issue clearly into focus:

> But Paul well knew that many who hear the gospel remain unbelievers. They may hear it with their ears, but it is not accepted as having any relevance for themselves, and so *is hid* as far as they are concerned. Paul is here stating in different language the teaching of Jesus in the parable of the sower. He is not implying that everyone who does not accept the gospel on any particular occasion is of necessity permanently *lost*, though, in some cases, this may be so. The Greek participle is more correctly translated "are perishing" as in RV and RSV. As long as men are on the road to perdition the gospel is veiled to them; and they are in this situation because of the activity of the *god of this world*.[5]

Nothing could be clearer here than the truth that the blindness of unbelievers is closely related to the work of Satan. The glorious light of the gospel penetrates this blindness. The issue here, again, is the presentation of the gospel, not the response to reasoned objections brought against the total system on which the gospel rests. When someone brings an objection to bear against Christian truth, it is imperative that the defender respond. God is certainly free; He is not bound by any of our preconceived patterns. He could certainly work in the mind of the lost person who objects to facets of Christian theism. He could even use arguments from the realm of apologetics as "preevangelism." However, only God in His sovereign grace and mercy can penetrate the darkness of unbelief. This truth cannot be compromised. By noting the distinctions between evangelism and apologetics, defenders of the faith can enter into vital contact with objectors, realizing that their activity of defense functions only within a circumscribed realm and is definitely not the same as evangelism.

Ephesians 4:17–18

"This I say therefore, and affirm together with the Lord, that you walk no longer just as the Gentiles also walk, in the futility of their mind, being darkened in their understanding, excluded from the life of God because of the ignorance that is in them, because of the hardness of their heart." These verses give a graphic description of life outside of Christ. They particularly show the way that pagans live during any time era and also reflect specifically on the way pagans lived in Paul's day. These verses imply moral and spiritual depravity on the part of the lost individuals of that day—or of any day. It is wrong to interpret these verses as implying that apologetics has no function, as if the darkened minds and warped understanding of unbelievers prevent them from grasping our answers. Again, the passage is clearly not aimed at negating apologetics, but at describing the total lifestyle of paganism. As Curtis Vaughan notes:

> The apostle proceeds to enumerate some of the salient features of pagan life in the first century: vanity, darkness, alienation, ignorance, hardness, loss of feeling, lasciviousness, uncleanness, greediness. It is a grim and revolting picture that he draws, in many respects parallel to the statement of Romans 1:18ff.
> First, Paul speaks of "the vanity of their mind" (vs. 17) and their being "darkened" in "the understanding" (vs. 18). "Vanity," a word often associated with idol worship, suggests emptiness, futility, and purposelessness—life with no real meaning, no goal. The thought is not that unregenerate minds are empty. It is that they are filled with things that lead to nothing. Cf. NEB, "good-for-nothing notions." To have "the understanding darkened" is to be without the faculty of discernment.[6]

The description of Ephesians 4:18b gives further evidence of the hopelessness of the unbeliever apart from the gracious action of God. "Ignorance" (Greek, *agnoian*) and "hardness of their heart" are the devastating terms used to describe the unregenerate. Again, notice that the "ignorance" described is based on the Greek word for knowing that implies experiential knowledge. Concerning "hardness," Vaughan points out that the Greek "word originally meant 'petrifaction' but came eventually to be used by medical writers of numbness, insensibility, callousness. Here it betokens an insensitivity to spiritual things . . . a 'steeling of the will against every good impulse.'"[7]

With this approach to the passage in mind, the student of apologetics recognizes the tragic condition of people apart from Christ; however, the defender is not daunted in efforts to give a cogent response to the objections raised against Christianity. He or she is free to speak, since Scripture gives no hint that the thought processes of the non-Christian in raising objections differ from the thought processes of the Christian in answering objections. The darkening of sin involves a clouding of the discerning process, so that the unregenerate person ultimately is seen as bound within the total implications of his or her system of thinking. Only God can break that bondage. This truth does not prohibit Christian defense, however. It simply puts it in proper perspective.

SUMMARY

No attempt has been made in this discussion to circumvent the careful teaching of Scripture about the lost condition of humanity. The truth of the total depravity of people is massive and must be seriously accepted. The passages dealt with here all show the radical need of people for the gospel of the grace of God. However, these passages do not negate the role of apologetics. Defenders of the faith gladly work within the strict guidelines of all Scripture in its sober and realistic evaluation of man's radical need.

REVIEW QUESTIONS

1. What does "common ground" mean in apologetics?
2. What common ground was suggested between the Christian defender and the non-Christian objector in the realm of communication?
3. Why is there a need to qualify the question of common ground at the level of classification?
4. What is meant by the statement that there is no common ground at the level of correlation?
5. How can it be shown that 1 Corinthians 1:17–31 does not restrict apologetics?
6. What was suggested as the main teaching point of 1 Corinthians 2:11?
7. How specifically does 1 Corinthians 2:14 show that there is a difference between perception and reception of truth?
8. What main truth does 1 Corinthians 2:11–14 explain?
9. Why can it be said that 2 Corinthians 4:3–4 does not rule out apologetics?
10. What is being described in Ephesians 4:17–18?

11. What exact meaning was suggested for the term *hardness* in Ephesians 4:18?

FOR FURTHER READING

Carnell, Edward J. "Common Ground." Chapter 12 in *An Introduction to Christian Apologetics: A Philosophic Defense of the Trinitarian-theistic Faith*. Grand Rapids: Eerdmans, 1948.

Lewis, Gordon R. *Testing Christianity's Truth-Claims: Approaches to Christian Apologetics*. Chicago: Moody, 1976. Pp. 13–36, 181–84.

Kingdon, D. P. "Depravity." In *Zondervan Pictorial Encyclopedia of the Bible*, edited by Merrill C. Tenney. Grand Rapids: Zondervan, 1975. Vol. 2, p. 102.

CHAPTER 7

The Challenge Concerning the Existence of God

After having laid down some ideas as to the nature and function of the apologetic task, we have come to the task of actually "doing apologetics." One does not have to look very far in the study of basic attitudes to come across atheism as a persistent and articulate rejection of truth about the existence of God. This challenge to Christianity cuts across many types of philosophical systems. As one Christian apologete has noted:

> Of course, atheism is not merely a negative position. Most atheists do not view themselves as antitheists but simply nontheists. As nontheists, atheists offer a positive view of their own which they may call humanism, materialism, naturalism or positivism.[1]

Our plan for this chapter will be, first, to look at various examples of the challenge against the truth of God's existence. Next, we will consider a biblical basis for theistic argumentation in response to atheism and other nontheistic voices. Finally, we will consider the relationship between revelation and reason as a further development of the groundwork of our response to nontheistic objections.

SOME EXAMPLES OF THE CHALLENGE

One school of thought that could be called naturalism sets itself over against Christian theism. It is easy to oversimplify here and to label as "naturalism" any nontheistic system that denies the supernatural. One philosopher notes:

Today naturalism has taken on a much wider meaning than that of materialism and positivism. In fact, its possibilities invite a great variety of metaphysical interpretation. This broadening of its area is a part of the widening visions of contemporary advocates who, although they see in the scientific temper the hope for a sound philosophical inquiry, are aware that there are areas in which nineteenth-century conceptions of science offered too limited views of the world.[2]

Naturalism is a broad term covering a particular attitude to philosophic inquiry. However, it can also be defined as a philosophy or complete way of looking at reality. A general description of this view puts the confrontation with Christian theism squarely into focus:

> Naturalism, challenging the cogency of the cosmological, teleological, and moral arguments, holds that the universe requires no supernatural cause and government, but is self-existent, self-explanatory, self-operating, and self-directing; that the world-process is not teleological and anthropocentric, but purposeless, deterministic . . . and only incidentally productive of man; that human life, physical, mental, moral and spiritual, is an ordinary natural event . . . and that man's ethical values, compulsions, activities, and restraints can be justified on natural grounds.[3]

The importance of this position for our study should not be missed. Whether it is called pragmatic naturalism or some other specific title, the crucial point is that it represents a nontheistic challenge to Christian theism.[4] One writer states:

> Unlike deism, naturalism has had great staying power. Born in the eighteenth century, it came of age in the nineteenth and grew to maturity in the twentieth. While signs of age are now appearing, naturalism is still very much alive. It dominates the universities, colleges and high schools. It provides the framework for most scientific study. It poses the backdrop against which the humanities continue to struggle for human value, as writers, poets, painters and artists in general shudder under its implications. No rival world view has yet been able to topple it, though it is fair to say that the twentieth century has provided some powerful options and theism is experiencing somewhat of a rebirth at all levels of society.[5]

Another system that offers objections to the truth of God's existence is humanism. Humanism as it is presently understood has some clear affinities to naturalism. In 1933 a group of humanists set forth what has come to be known as *Humanist Manifesto I*. This document was updated in 1973 and became known as *Humanist Manifesto II*. At point after point, the humanist view shows affinities with naturalism. Compare, for example, the introductory words in the description or definition of naturalism just given with these words from the *Humanist Manifesto*:

> *First:* Religious humanists regard the universe as self-existing and not created. . . . the nature of the universe depicted by modern science makes unacceptable any supernatural or cosmic guarantees of human values. . . . We are convinced that the time has passed for theism, deism, modernism, and the several varieties of "new thought."[6]

In the passing of forty years from 1933 to 1973, the humanist framework has not appreciably changed. That humanism and naturalism bear a distinct relationship becomes more apparent as these words from *Humanist Manifesto II* are studied:

> Any account of nature should pass the tests of scientific evidence; in our judgment, the dogmas and myths of traditional religions do not do so. . . . We find insufficient evidence for belief in the existence of a supernatural; it is either meaningless or irrelevant to the question of the survival and fulfillment of the human race. As non-theists, we begin with humans not God, nature not deity. Nature may indeed be broader and deeper than we now know; any new discoveries, however, will but enlarge our knowledge of the natural.[7]

Humanism gives attention to things that primarily affect people. It is a view that seeks to define happy and meaningful life for people within the framework of their own humanness, and it tries to give the means whereby people can achieve such a life, even in the light of the stark realities of nuclear power and international tensions.

Most of us probably will never actually be involved in a person-to-person debate with a philosopher who is oriented toward humanism or naturalism as an interpretation of life. However, we certainly might very well talk with individuals who give objections to Christianity based on the ideas they have heard from humanists, or perhaps read in their books, or even assumed from things they have learned in school at almost any level. The argumentation from nontheism hurls itself against the cogency of the arguments for God's existence, as noted in the description of naturalism stated earlier in this discussion. The response of Christian apologetics is to speak directly back to this argumentation. The basis for this response must be clearly delineated.

A BIBLICAL BASIS FOR THEISTIC ARGUMENTATION

There is a vast amount of literature on the subject of arguments for the existence of God. Speaking of several arguments of this type, W. G. T. Shedd noted:

> They assist the development of the idea of God, and contain a scientific analysis of man's natural consciousness of the deity. These arguments all derive their force from the innate idea, and the constitutional structure of man. . . . The human mind does not irrepressibly, and perpetually search for the evidence that a non-entity exists. 2. Secondly, these arguments reply to the counter-arguments of materialism and atheism.[8]

A more recent theologian calls these arguments "corroborations and expositions of our innate conviction of his existence."[9]

Romans 1:19–20 supplies an authoritative basis for man's understanding of truth about God, stating, "Because that which is known about God is evident within them; for God made it evident to them. For since the creation of the world His invisible attributes, His eternal power and divine nature, have been clearly seen, being understood through what has been made, so that they are without excuse."

This passage suggests the biblical basis for the truth about the innate idea of God *inside* the thinking process of every human being. The clause "that which is known about God is evident within them" has been the subject of debate as to its ultimate meaning. When the Bible says that this knowledge is manifest or "evident within them," it can as well read "among them" (Greek, *en autois*). This could imply that the knowledge was held *among* people, held in common, so to speak, by all of them. However, the word also surely would permit the idea that if this knowledge is held in common among people, there would have to be a ground of response *in each* one of them to receive this knowledge. A fitting summary of this idea can be found in these words: "We could say with more propriety: If there had been no general knowledge of God among them, there would have been no common guilt. We must admit, however, that *among them* pre-supposes *in them,* or the existence of a knowledge of God in their hearts."[10]

When the nontheist brings a reasoned objection against God, he or she is ultimately fighting against this truth. The defender of Christian truth must clearly understand this and balance the effort to give a response. The *reasons* or arguments for the existence of God, when presented carefully in this light, thus flow vitally and ulti-mately from the realm of truth, not error. There is truth to be known that God has revealed. God furthermore has vouchsafed this knowl-edge to the human race by giving His word—sacred Scripture. He also has set up the thinking or reasoning process, and this process is unified and universal for all human beings. At this point the regen-erate Christian defender of the truth can appeal to the fact that the *process* of reasoning and thinking is the same for the Christian and the non-Christian. It is the *framework* of thinking that differs for the two categories of people. The difference between the Christian and the non-Christian here is that the former has become obedient to the truth through the gracious action of God. The understanding of the Chrsitian has been freed from the bondage of a false orientation. The point here is crucial for apologetics. The truth about God as far as His existence goes is open to the thinking of all people. Furthermore, this truth moves in the realm of the understanding, the thinking process, and not just in the emotional life. This is seen by the fact that in Romans 1:20 the specific fact of God's knowledge in creation is re-vealed, and the area where it is to function is stated as in the human *reason.* Certainly, the human individual is a complex being (Ps. 139:14), and no intention here is given to separate the individual into convenient nonbiblical "parts." However, the term in Romans 1:20 precisely identifies the place where the truth of God found in crea-tion is to be understood. Notice the word I have italicized in the following quote from Romans 1:20: "His invisible attributes . . . have been clearly seen, being *understood* through what has been made." The emphasized word translates the Greek term *nooumena.* *Nous* (intellect), the Greek word for "mind," is directly seen in the very formation of *nooumena.* Thus the Bible designates the human understanding or thinking process as the place where the knowledge of God has been clearly seen and is continually being seen.

Consider now how the process of apologetics develops in a practical situation. Out of his or her thinking process the nontheist builds arguments against the cogency and relevancy of the statements or arguments for God's existence. Yet it is this very process of understanding or thinking, the rational process, that Scripture designates as the sphere, place, or realm where evidence of God's eternal power and divine nature can be seen. Thus the open invitation for the objector is to examine the evidence and, furthermore, to listen to the defense made in response to arguments against this evidence. To be sure, Romans 1:18–23 is not directed primarily to any philosophy or world view, but rather is directly explanatory as to the history and present condition of all the human race. To keep this as clear as possible, we must simply state that the Christian defender and the person who is raising objections about God's existence by questioning the evidence or inventing clever mental processes to deny the cogency of the arguments both *think* with the mind *(nous)*. They both think in a pattern of observation, analysis, and thought forms. Notice what Romans 1:20 does not state! It does not say, "being felt, or imagined, or dreamed," but it does say, "being understood." This is not to say that the feelings and total perceptive realm of people are invalid. But it does say that the place where evidence of some truth about God is to be dealt with is in the thinking, the understanding. Part of God's truth, namely, evidence for His existence involving His eternal power and divine nature (Rom. 1:20), is available to all and can be understood with the mind. Now the process of thinking that resists this will naturally invent every conceivable device to get away from the implications of God's revelation in creation and from God's truth in one's conscience or innate being. When seen in the light of being simply descriptions or tools to unfold this sphere of knowledge about God or to clarify it, the arguments for the existence of God become helps for explaining or clarifying the truth.

In summary, we can state that the internal revelation of God in the innate consciousness and in the mind or reasoning of man is balanced with an external revelation of truth unfolded in God's creation. It is necessary to delineate exactly what this revelation is. It is interesting to see how the Word of God sets forth the exact scope of this revelation of truth. God's Word states that through the "seeing" of thinking, understanding, and mental perception, certain "invisible" things (not perceived by sight) are discerned through the things that are made (Rom. 1:20). Pointedly, the text states that God's eternal power and divine nature are the two general things clearly seen continually in the things "made," or "through what has been made." *Theiotēs*, the Greek term translated "divine nature," seems to be a qualifying word, like "divinity," and characterizes the very nature of God. John Murray succinctly puts it as follows:

> Hence divinity does not specify one invisible attribute but the sum of the invisible perfections which characterize God. So, after all, the statement "eternal power and divinity" is inclusive of a great many invisible attributes and reflects on the richness of the manifestation given in the visible creation of the being, majesty, and glory of God.[11]

From this text there is a clear implication that phenomena in the world, things that are *finite* and observable, imply an *infinite* cause! This is true because of the terms "His eternal power and divine nature." These are clearly traits of the *infinite;* yet God sets up a thinking process and gives man the capacity to follow this thinking process. It seems clear that God Himself expects a process of thinking and reasoning that moves from created *finite* things to an intellectual perception of certain traits of His Being that are *infinite.* God's expectation of this perception can be seen in the words of Romans 1:20b: "so that they are without excuse."

This fits well into the pattern of apologetics. Reasoning from the created things, that is, "what has been made" (Rom. 1:20), is reasoning that moves into the pattern of the arguments for God's existence in a selective manner. John Murray states the implications of Romans 1:18–20:

> We must not tone down the teaching of the apostle in this passage. It is a clear declaration to the effect that the visible creation as God's handiwork makes manifest the invisible perfections of God as its Creator, that from the things which are perceptible to the senses cognition of these invisible perfections is derived, and that thus a clear apprehension of God's perfections may be gained from his observable handiwork. Phenomena disclose the noumena of God's transcendent perfec-

tion and specific divinity. It is not a finite cause that the work of creation manifests but the eternal power and divinity of the Creator. This is but another way of saying that God has left the imprints of his glory upon his handiwork and this glory is manifest to all—"God manifested it unto them" (vs. 19).[12]

REVELATION AND REASON

From the foregoing discussion we move to the subject of revelation and its relationship to reason. The ingredients for a balanced view of the relationship of these two elements are found in Scripture. This relationship can be stated as follows:

> It is a false contrast to polarize reason and revelation. They are not contradictories, contraries or even comparables. They are apples and oranges. Revelation is a means of communication (and secondarily that which is communicated); reason is the means of apprehension of what is communicated. Really the only means by which anything is communicated is revelation (unfolding or disclosing). The only way anything revealed is apprehended, grasped or understood is by reason. There is no other way of communication but by revelation. There is no other way of apprehension but by reason. Without revelation there would be no knowledge: without reason there would be no apprehension of knowledge.[13]

Romans 1:19–20 again speaks with force to this issue. Revelation, or the disclosure of truth from God, is given "through what has been made" (Rom. 1:20). Reason, or the ability to perceive such truth, is the reception of this revelation and is referred to explicitly in these words: "His invisible attributes, His eternal power and divine nature, *have been clearly seen, being understood* through what has been made." (Rom. 1:20, italics mine). When theistic argumentation is engaged in with the nontheist, or when statements of the truth of God's existence are presented, the activity can be described as an attempt to state very specific truth about God that is manifested in the things made, or in the realm of creation (nature). The attempt is to elucidate and clarify this process of thinking from the finite to the infinite that is expressed in the passage (see the quotation from Murray's commentary cited earlier).

Some of the misunderstanding about the relationship between revelation and reason comes from a failure to realize that all revelation is from God, whether it moves in the channel of creation or in the channel of Scripture. Louis Berkhof has commented on revelation as follows:

> In a certain sense it may be said that, according to Scripture, all revelation of God is supernatural, since it comes from God and reveals God, who possesses a life distinct from that of nature. As a rule the Bible does not trace the phenomena of nature to secondary causes, but to their primary cause, which is God or the will of God. The distinction was made rather early in history, however, but was not intended as a designation of a two-fold origin of revelation. It was clearly understood that all revelation of God is supernatural in origin, since it comes from God. It served rather to discriminate between two different modes of revelation. Natural revelation is communicated through the media of natural phenomena, while supernatural revelation implies a divine intervention in the natural course of events; it is supernatural not only in origin, but also in mode.[14]

Scripture clearly sets the limits on the evidence deposited in creation concerning the being of God. The truth stands, as Romans 1:20 states, in the undeniable evidence for God's eternal power and divine nature. Furthermore, Scripture itself is the clear and authoritative interpretation of what evidence is open to reason here. The place of theistic argumentation is to function squarely within this scriptural pattern of Romans 1:20, and not to step beyond this circumscribed area. As one theologian has noted, the limitations of truth revealed in creation are set:

> But there are a great number of supremely important truths that the material universe can never reveal to the searching eye of man, even if he could bring an unfallen mind and a pure heart to the investigation of its wonders. It is for this reason that God, in His infinite grace and love, has given us in the Bible the *supreme and only authoritative revelation* concerning the Persons of the Trinity, the original creation, the nature of man, the Fall and Edenic curse, the Tower of Babel, the Abrahamic and Mosaic covenants, the miracles of Moses, Elijah, and other prophets, the incarnation, atoning death, and bodily resurrection of Christ, the nature and purpose of the Church, the unseen world of spirit beings (including Satan), the Second Coming of Christ, the future judgments, heaven and hell, and many other vitally important truths.[15]

Table 2 illustrates the possible comparison of the revelation of truth about God in Creation and the truth about God in Scripture.

TABLE 2
REVELATION: COMMUNICATION FROM GOD

The channel or mode of creation (nature)	The channel or mode of Scripture (the Word of God)
Truth seen clearly (Rom. 1:20) in the phenomena of creation	Truth inerrantly stated in the entire Scriptures
God's eternal power and divine nature	God's eternal love and grace
Specific truth about the being and nature of God	Specific truth about the total Trinitarian being and existence of God and His redemptive plan
Truth in this realm can be acknowledged through the thinking process;	Truth in this realm can be appropriated through obedient faith (which includes thought *(notitia)*;
Reason can perceive the truth of the God of creation	Reason can and does repose in and rest on the truth of the God of creation

When revelation is seen in this light, there is no false bifurcation of truth revealed from God. There is no scriptural warrant for limiting the power of God's revelation. Each channel can be seen as functioning within the biblical guidelines.

In the next chapter we will examine selectively some of the reasons or arguments for the existence of God that form key issues in the nontheist/Christian confrontation.

REVIEW QUESTIONS

1. In the general description of naturalism, what does naturalism state about the universe?
2. What signs can be given to demonstrate the fact that naturalism is still very much alive?
3. What do the more recent humanists postulate about the existence of God?
4. What is the meaning of the clause "that which is known about God is evident within them" (Rom. 1:19)?
5. What is the difference between the Christian and the non-Christian in regard to reasoning and thinking?
6. How can Romans 1:20 specifically show that the place where the knowledge of God is to be manifested is in the mind or thinking process, and not just in the emotions?

7. What terms in Romans 1:20 imply a process of thinking from finite things to infinite causation or infinite things?

8. State concisely the relationship between reason and revelation.

9. Compare concisely the channel or mode of revelation in creation (nature) and the mode of revelation in Scripture.

FOR FURTHER READING

Brown, Colin. *Philosophy and the Christian Faith: A Historical Sketch From the Middle Ages to the Present Day*. Downers Grove, Ill.: InterVarsity, 1968. Pp. 132–51.

Geisler, Norman L., and Feinberg, Paul. "The Relationship Between Faith and Reason." Chap. 17 in *Introduction to Philosophy: A Christian Perspective*. Grand Rapids: Baker, 1980.

Gerstner, John H. "Reason and Revelation." *Tenth: An Evangelical Quarterly* vol. 9, no. 4 (October 1979), p. 26.

Ramm, Bernard. *Protestant Christian Evidences*. Chicago: Moody, 1953. Chapter 2, pp. 45–80.

Sire, James W. *The Universe Next Door: A Basic World View Catalog*. Downers Grove, Ill.: InterVarsity, 1976. Chap. 4, pp. 58–75.

CHAPTER 8

Some Arguments
for Theism

We are now ready to consider some challenges from nontheism concerning various arguments for the existence of God. An attempt will be made here to examine selectively some of these arguments and then to put them into a framework for the defense of Christian theism. We will omit the ontological argument from the classical argumentation for God's existence, for it seems to differ substantially from the three others we will consider. As noted in the previous chapter, the arguments for the existence of God can be viewed as a way of developing and unfolding the biblical truth of Romans 1:18–21. Inasmuch as the ontological argument does not move from phenomena, but rather from other grounds, it seems wise to deal only with the cosmological, teleological, and moral arguments in this discussion.

THE COSMOLOGICAL ARGUMENT

The Statement of the Argument

The argument has been well stated by a humanist, Hector Hawton. He knows the position of theism well, having formerly become a theist and having practiced this belief for some years. However, he later rejected this position and became a humanist. He writes:

> The arguments run as follows: We can observe, for example, that every effect is preceded by a cause, therefore unless we admit an infinite

regress, there must be a First Cause. Similarly, we find order in Nature, and this cannot have arisen by chance; there must be an Orderer. . . . Many people vaguely feel that there *must* be an explanation on these lines and "God" seems to fill the gap. It is because of this inarticulate feeling that explicit atheism is confined to a small minority, though religion is in decline and people who shrink from denying that God exists, carry on as though he did not. . . . Something must have started it all, people feel, when they look up at the stars. This "something" is at the heart of the Cosmological Argument.[1]

The cosmological argument can be illustrated by a statement from Scripture. Although this is not the primary interpretation of Hebrews 3:4, this text reflects the movement of thought in this argument: "For every house is built by someone, but the builder of all things is God." Every existing thing in the world must have an adequate cause. If this is so, the universe must therefore also have an adequate cause. The term *cosmological* is made up of the Greek words *cosmos* ("world") and *logos* ("discourse about, "word," or "reason").

Objections to the Argument

The nontheist offers very specific and detailed objections to this argument. Thus Bertrand Russell, for example, gives the following response from naturalism to this argument:

If everything must have a cause, then God must have a cause. If there can be anything without a cause, it may just as well be the world as God, so that there cannot be any validity in that argument. It is exactly of the same nature as the Hindu's view, that the world rested upon an elephant and the elephant rested upon a tortoise; and when they said, "How about the tortoise?" the Indian said, "Suppose we change the subject." The argument is really no better than that. There is no reason why the world could not have come into being without a cause; nor, on the other hand, is there any reason why it should not have always existed. There is no reason to suppose that the world had a beginning at all. The idea that things must have a beginning is really due to the poverty of our imagination.[2]

The Cosmological Argument Restudied

Defenders of the validity of the cosmological argument have articulated detailed answers to its critics.[3] Contrary to Russell's idea as stated above, there is every reason to understand that the world had a beginning. The second law of thermodynamics establishes the concept that the universe is running down, and the reasonable inference from this concept is that it must have had a beginning.[4] This law directly refutes the thinking that Russell propounded in his rejection of the cosmological argument. Morris has stated the implications of the law for theistic argumentation:

> The Second Law implies that, if present processes continue, the universe will become completely "dead" in time. If it were *infinitely* old, it would already be dead. Thus, in its present form, it must have had a beginning! The First Law, however, indicates that it could not have created itself. It must, therefore, have been created by a Creator outside itself and by processes of creation which are not now occurring, exactly as the creation model postulates.
>
> This evidence does not necessarily *prove* creation to be true. It is conceivable that a naturalistic integrative process might have occurred . . . or that such a process might even today be occurring in that part of the universe outside the *known* universe. In *observable* space and time, however, there is no such thing. Science is what we *see,* and we see only a universal disintegrative process pointing back to an initial creation.[5]

Critics of the cosmological argument suggest that arguing back from effect to cause will not lead to an infinite and external causation force. They state, rather, that there will simply be an infinite regress of cause and effect backwards into time, so to speak, and that this cycle cannot be used to shift gears perceptually to an infinite Creator who is the ultimate uncaused Being. The appeal to "infinite regress" is, however, itself open to question. It might be a two-edged sword in a sense, for, as Ferre points out,

> the fact remains that infinite regress is not so much an explanation as a rejection of the demand for an explanation. And as such it poses a mortal threat to scientific as well as metaphysical investigation. Both metaphysics and science exist within, depend upon, man's questing, curious impulses; and appeal to infinite regress is, if successful, curiosity's assassin. The mind may be hypnotized into passivity by staring back, and back, and back . . . into the endless depths of time, but this is no way to obtain a sufficient explanation for any specific question.[6]

The point here should be obvious. Observed phenomena stand in the creation as open avenues of interpretation. Causation functions, despite Russell's feelings to the contrary, and the implications of the second law of thermodynamics are critical for this discussion. To start with, something that is uncaused, "a first cause alone answers truly to the idea of a cause. A secondary cause, in so far as secondary, in so far as caused, is not a cause."[7]

The one who theorizes that the world could have come into being without a cause is saying simply and logically that it is self-caused, or self-created. The Christian apologete can ask in response: How could the universe have caused itself to come into being? How could the universe have created itself? Logically, to say that something is self-caused is to imply the prior existence of the self to cause itself! To create means to originate or to bring into being. R. C. Sproul succinctly responds to the idea of a self-caused world this way:

> What is wrong with the notion of self-creation? What would have to happen for something to create itself? Obviously, for something to create itself, it would have to exist in order to create. It would have to exist before it existed if it were to create its own existence. Are you getting a headache? For something to create itself it would have to be and not be at the same time and have the same relationship. To do that it would have to violate the law basic to all science, the law of contradiction. To say that something exists and does not exist at the same time and in the same way is to make a nonsense statement. The notion of self-creation is irrational in the extreme.[8]

To say that the world had no beginning is the same thing ultimately as saying that matter, the material or "stuff" of which the universe is made, is eternal. Here again, Christian apologetes ask the nontheist to carry this idea out to its logical conclusion. Remember that Christian apologetics are carried on with the full realization that the process of thinking can be engaged in with the non-Christian on the common ground of communication. Both the Christian and the non-Christian have the same method of constructing and receiving statements about reality. Certainly, the non-Christian will not be convinced of the truth of Christianity until God graciously works in the total person, including the understanding, emotions, heart, and mind. But on the common ground of thinking about reality, the Christian defender challenges the very concept of the eternity of matter. Christian apologete John H. Gerstner says:

Matter is an effect, produced by an adequate cause. Clearly, that which is itself an effect cannot be the cause of all things. . . . Matter may, in some sense, be a cause, but it also is an effect. That which is an effect cannot itself be the first cause. And only the first cause was in the beginning.

But how do we know that matter is an effect, and not a first cause? If matter were the author of all things, it would be, in the first place, the author of life. But how can it be? Matter itself has no life. It is, by definition, "inanimate."[9]

There is a careful response to be given on the really basic question of the beginning of all of life and the power behind the scenes, so to speak. The cosmological argument moves forward along the line of thinking about the origin of the universe; it necessarily concerns itself with *power* sufficient to explain the totality of reality, including all matter, as well as the existence of life and living beings. At this point in the defense, the Christian can urge the non-Christian to look at the trustworthy and reliable record of Scripture, which makes many striking and openly verifiable claims. Scripture does not attempt to prove the existence of God directly, for He must be apprehended by faith (Heb. 11:6). However, there is evidence of His existence and activity all through the Bible, as for example in the record of the origin of the universe. As he uses the cosmological argument, the apologete should keep in mind that the yearnings of the innate consciousness that are present in varying degrees in all people, even called "finitude," a sense of dependence or need, in the face of the *cosmos,* are ultimately explained by such passages of Scripture as Romans 1:18–21; Psalm 19:1–6; and Acts 17:24–31. In the truth stated in these passages is found the ultimate interpretation to the *power* source behind the universe. This is the uncaused Being, the God of the ages, of whom Scripture states, "In the beginning God created the heavens and the earth" (Gen. 1:1).

The cosmological argument can provide fitting and appropriate groundwork for the defense of the faith. Its pattern of thinking can be shown to function within the guidelines of Romans 1:20. A modern statement of the argument, offered by Norman L. Geisler, can be charted as follows:

OPTIONS FOR ULTIMATE STARTING POINTS OF THE UNIVERSE	PROBLEMS WITH EACH OPTION
1. The universe is self-caused.	1. Impossible. It cannot give existence to itself, for that implies it has existence already.
2. The ultimate or basic cause of the universe is, in turn, caused by another.	2. Impossible. It is the ultimate or first cause alone that has no causes behind or beyond it.

The conclusion offered here is as follows:

A *self*-caused being is impossible, but an *un*caused Being is not.

Further, it is as an uncaused Cause that the essential metaphysical attributes of this Cause can be unpacked to identify it with the God of the Judeo-Christian tradition. Let us move directly to unpack what is implied in an uncaused Cause of the existence of finite, limited, changing beings.[10]

It is crucial for this discussion to reiterate the clear implications of Romans 1:20. Apparently God Himself intended man as a thinking being to be able to think back from contingency and finiteness to an infinite Cause, an uncaused Cause, as we have already established. Thus the entire matter is concluded fittingly with these words:

In fact, it is undeniably true that something exists that need not exist (e.g., myself). Therefore, since something exists, it is ontologically necessary that something exists as a ground for all contingent existence. The existence of contingent beings demands a necessary Being on which they can be contingent. For if the contingent beings are caused beings, then the uncaused Cause of these beings must be a noncontingent Being, i.e., a necessary Being.[11]

THE TELEOLOGICAL ARGUMENT

The Statement of the Argument

The name reveals the direction of the argument. *Teleological* is composed of the Greek words *telos* ("purpose") and *logos* ("discourse about," "reasoning"). The teleological argument stresses *purpose* or design in the universe and invites careful thinking about this subject. Psalm 94:9 illustrates the pattern of thinking though this verse does not directly teach the teleological argument. Psalm 94:9

states, "He who planted the ear, does He not hear? He who formed the eye, does He not see?" Certainly, this verse could include in its breadth of meaning the reality that the intricate auditory mechanism, for example, forms a basis for reflecting on an intelligent, purposeful Being who, at an infinite level, is capable of assimilating information, even as human beings do hear things at a finite level.

The illustrations of design and purpose in the universe are plentiful. Theologian James O. Buswell, Jr., notes that

> the inorganic world is marvelously adapted for the preservation of life. It seems highly improbable that any other planet in the universe is arranged for the purposes of life as this planet is. The axis of the earth being at an angle to the plane of the ecliptic, the light and heat of the sun are distributed over the earth in the changing seasons. The blanket of the air preserves the earth from extremes of temperature. In innumerable other ways this earth looks as though it were made for the purposes of life. . . . An atheistic professor once told me of visiting the Hoover Dam in the gorge of the Colorado River. He said that his wife, in observing the formations of the rocks, kept saying, "What wonderful works of God!" Finally his ten-year-old boy replied to his mother, "Well, Mom, the rocks had to fall somewhere, didn't they?"
>
> I asked the atheist if he had seen the dam itself. "Oh yes," he replied; and he was quite enthusiastic over the remarkable engineering of the structure. I asked about the great quantities and varieties of materials used in the dam, and the atheist expanded his description.
>
> Finally I asked him, "When you saw the Hoover Dam with all these materials and their remarkable arrangement, did you say to yourself, 'Well, these things had to fall somewhere, didn't they?'" To this he had no reply.[12]

Objections to the Teleological Argument

The nontheist rejects the cogency of this argument also. Certainly, many objections have been raised, but they cannot all be cited in this study. One objection rests on the modern era of science and the general acceptance of the theory of evolution. As long as the philosophy of materialism (matter in motion) was prevalent, the argument from design seemed valid. The movement of the astral bodies in an orderly fashion seemed to give the impression of a cosmic clock and pointed back to the Creator of this kind of order. But modern science, so the argument goes, particularly in the realm of biology, has rejected design and accepted rather the idea of natural selection in the pattern of development. For the naturalist, this seems to mitigate the idea of any purpose or cosmic Mind in control. This position has been summarized as follows:

> There is no need to look for some agency outside the physical world. The conditions in which life emerged on this planet are a certain range of temperature, and certain chemical combinations which, it is widely believed today—though it was not some thirty or forty years ago—are probably found on numerous planets throughout this vast universe. The variations which gave rise to a multiplicity of species are due to mutations in the genetic material. . . . The feeling that the world around us *looks* as though it had been deliberately designed is very deep, but it will not bear critical examination.[13]

A Response to Objections to the Teleological Argument

As seen in the previously cited material, nontheists assign to mutations the functional process of explaining diversity and development in the complex patterns of living beings. Technically speaking, a mutation is "any heritable alteration of the genes or chromosomes of an organism."[14] Specifically, from the non-Christian perspective, instead of order there is randomness, and instead of design there is simply natural selection with a mechanism of mutations to explain the different species. There is a built-in problem with this explanation. Most mutations are harmful and destructive. The naturalist framework here depends on a process that for the most part does not produce positive variation, but rather negative and even harmful degeneration. Amazingly, after postulating mutations as the basis for variation, Hector Hawton gives evidence of feeling that they are still adequate to explain the multiplicity of the species, even though they are harmful.[15]

Instead of purpose, most naturalists accept chance as the only acceptable alternative to order and design. In response to this, the apologete can point out that it is demonstrable that the chances of life simply happening at random are so remotely and statistically improbable that there is no way to really appeal to chance as an adequate explanation for design and purpose. The time-worn illustration about the explanation of Webster's dictionary still holds true, as Charles F. Baker notes:

It is very difficult to believe that blind chance could have produced this intricate balance in all realms of nature. One scientist, commenting upon this point, has said that there would be as much probability of chance producing a universe of order such as we see around us as an explosion in a type-foundry producing *Webster's Unabridged Dictionary*.[16]

In summary it can be noted that the evidence for design and purpose form, even in the recent era, fitting avenues for the defense of faith.

THE MORAL OR ANTHROPOLOGICAL ARGUMENT

The Statement of the Argument

Though variously presented, the argument posits the existence of an intelligent and moral Being to explain the existence of people. Thus the discourse or reasoning or word (Greek, *logos*) about man (*anthropos*) can lead to a consideration of their Creator. Stressing the nature of people as sentient beings with a will, reasoning powers, and emotions, some Christian theists speak back to the challenge of naturalism and stress the validity of this anthropological or moral argument. Stated in one form, the very fact that a person feels he or she "ought" to act in a certain manner implies a responsible Agent or Source for that deep-seated sense of responsibility. In other words Someone exists who says, "You shall act in such a manner" in response to the innate feeling expressed in such terms as "I ought to do this." This argument then infers a Person who speaks and sets down intelligent patterns for life and behavior. Pehaps the full implication of this argument is the concept that it points to a Person able to account for man as a total and complex being who must function in a morally responsible manner.

The moral argument can be seen by applying some of the truths revealed in Romans 2:14–15. Again, a detailed study of the passage will reveal that Paul is not presenting the moral argument as such. Rather, he notes that a representative spectrum of the human race, the Gentiles, is seen as instinctively functioning according to a standard. The words of Scripture that follow reveal this direction of a standard and norm for action: "For when Gentiles who do not have the Law do instinctively the things of the Law, these, not having the

Law, are a law to themselves, in that they show the work of the Law written in their hearts, their conscience bearing witness, and their thoughts alternately accusing or else defending them" (Rom. 2:14–15). Moving in and around the idea of conscience and ethical action, the Christian apologete can use the moral argument against the challenge of naturalism. He can explain that only Christian theism as unfolded properly in its biblical dimension can ultimately give full meaning to a person's complex existence and moral nature.

The Moral Argument Challenged

The point of challenge here is directed at the core of the argument. The naturalist does not postulate any kind of Lawgiver. All human behavior arose from the evolutionary process, according to naturalism, and all sense of "ought-ness" in human behavior can be explained on this basis. The challenge is stated forthrightly here:

> The belief in a moral law—and therefore in a divine Lawgiver—is a survival from those ancient civilizations which made no distinction between laws of Nature and morality. A breach of the moral law was believed to disturb the very course of Nature, bringing pestilence, famine and drought as a punishment. This line of thought is no less anachronistic when it is expressed in more refined language. . . . a purely naturalistic explanation can be given of the differences we find in moral codes, and of the conviction we feel that our own values are absolutely binding. . . . Whether conscience is actually the product of a social conditioning or of an infantile attitude to a parent—the Freudian super-ego—it is in either case an entirely natural development. There is no longer any need to look for a transcendental cause.[17]

The Moral Argument Stated in Response to Criticism

C. S. Lewis stressed the careful statement of the moral argument in his defense of Christian truth. He engaged in detailed interaction with the criticism brought against the argument. The first five chapters of his work *Mere Christianity* offered a pathway of thinking to show that there is a universal moral law that cannot be traced to herd instinct, mere convention, some indescribable "law of nature," or mere imaginative "fancy." The final summary of this statement of the moral argument has been carefully summarized and synthesized as follows:

Therefore, there is an absolutely perfect power outside of mankind which is more like mind than anything we know, since—

a. It gives us moral commands.

b. It is very much interested in our behavior (i.e., in the keeping of these commands).

c. If it were not absolutely good, then all moral effort would be futile in the long run (e.g., we may be sacrificing our lives for the vain cause of "right" unless there is really an absolute "right").

d. This source of all right must be absolutely good, for the standard for all good cannot be less than completely good himself).[18]

The Christian theist asks the objector to reflect and critically evaluate his or her own position with the same kind of critical thinking that has been leveled against theism. Driven back to ultimates, naturalists are faced with some rather devastating problems. First, in their viewpoint the entire universe arose through the mechanism of chance. Second, inorganic and organic phenomena arose purely by chance. Third, organic phenomena, through countless millions of years, evolved into units approximating the present phylogenetic "tree of life," with myriads of differentiations, one of them *homo sapiens,* man, who can think, reflect, and even meditate about the fact that he can reflect and think! Fourth, this kind of life, human life, then develops codes of behavior, apparently totally by the process of trial and error. A person who reflects for a moment about the seriousness of this might wonder, What about the dimension of "telling the truth"? The conclusions of the naturalist are written down and presented to readers in an attempt to function within a norm of "truth telling." It is an appeal to some kind of standard or norm to expect readers and hearers of great issues involving a comparison of world views to decide upon the "rightness" or "wrongness" of truth claims. Yet, given the vantage point of naturalism concerning the ultimate nature of man, how can naturalists be sure they have arrived at anything when they make definitive statements about reality, or even statements that imply there is no truth? At best, it seems that a rather hopeless sense of futility would drive the reflective naturalist to a position of simply hoping to gain the best by a process of doing what is of value to the most people for the very survival of the race.

Instead of demonstrating that the moral argument has no cogency, adherents of naturalism appeal to almost authoritarian and even dogmatic statements that seemingly defy the very logic they hope to use as the test for all truth. For example, Bertrand Russell, in his famous essay "Why I Am Not a Christian" objected to the moral argument. He constructed a pattern of thinking that moved forward step by step to end up with his rejection of God's existence. The steps are these:

1. There can be no right or wrong unless God exists, say Christians.

2. Christians further say that there is a radical difference between right and wrong.

3. Christians say that God Himself, as to His nature, is good (conforming to right, in other words, not wrong).

4. As soon as Christians say this, they really admit that right and wrong have some meaning that is independent of God or of God's fiat (plan, decree, or order). In other words, the only way someone can classify God as being "good" would be to understand that "goodness" or "badness" as classifications cannot come from God; therefore, Christians really cannot argue back to God's existence prior to anything else. Good and evil must have independent existence. Russell put it this way:

> "If you are going to say, as theologians do, that God is good, you must then say that right and wrong have some meaning which is independent of God's fiat, because God's fiats are good and not bad independently of the mere fact that he made them. If you are going to say that, you will then have to say that it is not only through God that right and wrong came into being, but that they are in their essence logically anterior to God.[19]

These statements are put forth cogently and carefully by Russell. They are either true or false. They must be tested and answered. In giving answer to the statements, the same kind or process of thinking can be followed. The same "raw materials" and ideas will be dealt with. Russell's position cannot stand in the face of straight thinking. Let us take the steps that he followed one at a time and subject them to critical analysis.

1. There is a difference between God's nature and being, and His plan, blueprint or purpose (Russell used the word *fiat*).

2. On the ground of Christian theism, nothing whatever, other than the Triune Godhead, existed prior to creation.

3. God created all things, man included, by fiat, plan, or decree.

4. True "goodness" is conformity to God's will or decree.

5. In the decree God purposed to create, to give existence to, intelligent beings—angels and human beings.

6. Thus God's decree, fiat, or plan itself included beings who themselves ultimately produced action contrary to the goodness of God. As Francis Schaeffer states:

> It is perfectly true that in making man as he did God made the possibility of evil. But the bare possibility of evil is not the actualizing of it. And in making that possibility, God validated choice and validated man as man—a being significant in history. If he had left him without choice, you could speak forever of man being man, man being significant, but it would be only meaningless words.[20]

7. Thus good and evil are not "logically anterior" to God. God's *nature* or Being is good, but His *plan* includes both good and evil. Evil is *actualized;* it is certainly within the knowledge of God and is permitted by Him but it is not produced by Him.

Christian apologetics functions at this level of interchange with Russell's ideas, which fall short of cogency. Russell does not differentiate between God and His plan—between God's being, or nature, and His will or program. If the nontheist can understand the objections raised by Russell, he or she can understand the answer here. The defender of the faith invites the naturalist to think along a different pattern, so to speak. At this point the case is simply stated and rested. However, the issue is far deeper. Arguments are propounded by human beings, real people, with real life and existence. These individuals are not simply objects to be answered, that is, "cut down" to logical size. Rather, they are individuals for whom Christ died. Thus the intense desire on the part of Christians is really far more than to give intellectual answers to naturalists. When the Christian engages in the *action* of apologetics, an *attitude* of concern for individuals will most assuredly include an *attitude* of evangelism. W. L. Craig, a modern defender of the faith, has summarized this balance accurately in the preface of a book dealing with detailed argumentation on God's existence. He writes:

In this book I will share with you several arguments which I consider convincing in an attempt to show you that God exists. Should my arguments seem weak and unconvincing to you, that is my fault, not God's. It only shows that I am a poor philosopher, not that God does not exist. Whether you judge my arguments to be sound or fallacious, God still exists; He loves you and holds you accountable. I will do my best to present sound arguments to you. But ultimately you must deal, not with arguments, but with God Himself.[21]

SUMMARY AND CONCLUSION

Someone might well wonder why everyone is not convinced if the flow of straight thinking always can be shown to validate the Christian's belief in God. The answer to this question involves the deeper needs of man's heart. Sin and the rejection of God and His truth are far deeper than the mind or thinking framework alone. The obvious issue is that the entire will of the naturalist or naturalist-influenced person is set against the truth. Thus the Christian defender of the truth is all the more bound not to expect the defense made against naturalism's arguments about God to accomplish more than what is biblical. Scripture sets the purpose of God's revelation in His creation. Interestingly enough, the statement of Romans 1:20 could easily be seen as a definitive or final apologetic to the minds of people. The text clearly implies that the *finite* phenomena of the universe point to truth about the *infinite* Creator. The purpose for this is that "they are without excuse" (Greek, *anapologētous*). Notice closely the word *anapologētous*. In its very construction is the term *apologetic* (response, defense). The Greek word, with a compound prefix, simply means "without defense, without apology." The point is that God's revelation in creation stands as an ongoing confrontation with the human race. If people reject this evidence, they are "without defense," that is, they have no apologetic or final defense against this evidence in their responsibility to acknowledge truth.

The arguments offered have been in response to some of the nontheists' objections to an interpretation of evidence for God's existence. The Christian defender of the faith simply speaks back to the objections, offering defense in this manner. In his comments on Hebrews 11:6, Philip E. Hughes has given a fitting summary to the work of this chapter:

Throughout the whole of Scripture the existence of God is never a matter of doubt or debate. Such reasonings as are found (for example, Ps. 19:1ff.; Rom. 1:19ff.) always start from assurance, never from uncertainty. God is not a metaphysical concept for questioning and discussion. He is the supreme reality, and the foundation and source of all created being. Hence when the reader is advised that to draw near to God he *must believe that he exists* he is not being invited to take a step in the dark but to turn to the light; he is not being encouraged to work up a blind faith but to entrust the whole of his being to him who is himself truth and light and life.[22]

REVIEW QUESTIONS

1. State concisely the cosmological argument.

2. What can the second law of thermodynamics imply for the notion that the world has always existed?

3. What exactly is wrong with saying that the universe is self-caused or self-created?

4. What is the teleological argument?

5. What is wrong with suggesting that chance could be an explanation for life's origin rather than God?

6. What is the moral argument?

7. How specifically is the moral argument challenged by a purely naturalistic explanation?

8. State in brief summary form Bertrand Russell's objection to the moral argument.

9. State in contrast the suggested response to Russell here. How does differentiating correctly between God's nature and His plan or fiat help in clarifying the issue?

10. Why is not everyone convinced about the truth of God's existence if this can be demonstrated by a process of straight thinking?

FOR FURTHER READING

Buswell, James O., Jr. *A Systematic Theology of the Christian Religion*. Grand Rapids: Zondervan, 1962. Vol. 1, pp. 72–101.

Craig, William Lane. *The Existence of God and the Beginning of the Universe*. San Bernardino, Calif.: Here's Life Publications, 1979.

Geisler, Norman L. *Christian Apologetics*. Grand Rapids: Baker, 1976. Pp. 215–59.

———. *Philosophy of Religion*. Grand Rapids: Zondervan, 1974. Pp. 87–132, 163–226.

Gerstner, John H. *Reasons for Faith*. Grand Rapids: Baker, 1967. Pp. 23–57.

Ramm, Bernard L. *The God Who Makes a Difference: A Christian Appeal to Reason*. Waco: Word, 1972. Pp. 77–118.

Sproul, R. C. *If There Is a God, Why Are There Atheists?* Minneapolis: Bethany Fellowship, 1978. Pp. 9–80.

_____. *Objections Answered*. Glendale, Calif.: G/L Publications, 1978. Pp. 87–103.

Shedd, W. G. T. *Dogmatic Theology*. 1876. Reprint. Grand Rapids: Zondervan, 1976. Pp. 195–248.

CHAPTER 9

An Apologetic Method
and a Pattern of Vindication

INTRODUCTION

In defending Christian theism, we challenged the cogency of some of the objections to the classic arguments for the existence of God. However, this is only one avenue of defense. It is certainly not all there is to apologetics with reference to naturalism or other systems of interpreting the world that are opposed to Christianity.

AN APOLOGETIC METHOD

It is vital now to give a step-by-step study of an apologetic method that can be used for any defense of the faith as set over against systems of thinking opposed to Christianity. For the sake of clarity, each step will be identified and then briefly explained.

Information

The first step in responding to a position that clashes with Christian theism is to learn exactly what the builders of that system of thought believe. This involves a serious attempt to gain information and to understand the main ideas, starting points, or presuppositions on which the system is based. Behind the scenes of every idea presented for interpreting reality, there rests a basic position or philosophy. If we are to function within the biblical guidelines of contending earnestly for the faith (Jude 3), we will find that one aspect of this work consists of knowing what we are contending with.

Systematization

Second, it is imperative that the ideas of the position being studied be understood clearly, stated clearly and fairly, and organized into some kind of working pattern or system. Where possible, the Christian apologete should seek to identify sources or authors who are aware of what Christian theism is and what Christianity teaches but still have set themselves against the Christian position. By doing this the Christian can be sure that he or she is studying and responding to the best possible statement of non-Christian ideologies.

Confrontation

Third, the Christian apologete should identify the tensions between the system in question and Christianity. He should be sure that the major issues or questions come clearly into focus. Most assuredly there will be a diligent and even creative use of Scripture at this point as well as throughout the entire defense. The defender of the Christian faith must have a growing and maturing use and understanding of the Bible and of biblical principles that reveal the depth of Christian theism as opposed to the shortcomings of other systems of thought. At this point of actual confrontation, biblical truth must be stated against the system in question, and that truth must be based on the process of sound thinking that God Himself established, for God is the author of all truth and all the processes of sound thinking. It is in the stage of confrontation that Christian apologetics carries on its most unique action. As answers are given to the points of tension within the system being studied, doubtless there will be other corollary questions that come into view. Perhaps the activity here of confronting the non-Christian position on a continuing basis can be likened to Paul's activity in continuing to reason with Felix, as described in Acts 24:25–27. Certainly the situations of modern defense and Paul's relationship to Felix are radically different. Yet there are principles in Scripture that govern our pattern of apologetics, and there are some guidelines that we can apply from this kind of interaction with non-Christian systems of thought. Paul called attention very pointedly to truth about the Christian system—specifically to truth on which the gospel is built—when he "was discussing righteousness, self-control and the judgment to come" (Acts 24:25a). These issues had great personal relevance to Felix and Drusilla. They are truths inherent in Christian theism and involve man's responsibility to the God of creation. The term *discussing* in Acts 24:25 gives at least a hint of the method for Christian proclamation and defense in the modern era. The proclamation of the gospel had been made. Further clarifications of truths inherent in the Christian theistic system were doubtless openly explained in Paul's ongoing discussions with Felix. Here, then, is a possible pattern for continuing the dialogue with nontheists.

Implication

Fourth, the Christian apologete must take the non-Christian presuppositions to their ultimate implication and result. Many times individuals influenced by naturalism or humanism, for example, do not really isolate and identify their own presuppositions and carry them through to their logical conclusions. The naturalist needs to be faced with the rather staggering assumptions, for example, of the origin of all life on the ground of chance (without getting into the technicalities of arguing whether it is mathematical chance or philosophical chance). He or she needs to face the stark reality of all things beginning from point zero with no basis for postulating even the rise of mechanisms or the continuance of mechanisms to keep the symmetry or order in life. The very minimum that the Christian apologete should do is to confront the naturalist with the ultimate truth that that position is essentially a commitment of *believing* something to be true with a philosophical commitment, not a commitment based on evidence. The point we make here is that Christian theism, by contrast, rests on documented evidence, the written Word of God, and this evidence openly invites the observer and student of human history and life and meaning to examine it as a complete system of truth with respect to all of reality. Building on such a process of thinking as this, the Christian apologete can at least point the objector to a consideration of origins, reality, and life as revealed in the Bible. In inviting the objector to investigate these truths, the defender can point out that the Bible makes the astounding claim to be an authentic interpretation of the reality that the naturalist claims is self-explanatory, self-directed, and purposeless!

Explanation

Often Christianity is misrepresented or misunderstood by its critics. An example of this can be found in the ideas that Bertrand Russell had about the basis of Christianity. He believed that fear or terror of the unknown drove people to invent religion (by this broad term he included Christianity) with its ideas of a power or force beyond human life, something or someone who would be able to help in time of troubles and fears. He summarized this hard criticism with these words:

> Religion is based, I think, primarily and mainly upon fear. It is partly the terror of the unknown . . . fear of the mysterious, fear of defeat, fear of death. Fear is the parent of cruelty, and therefore it is no wonder if cruelty and religion have gone hand in hand. It is because fear is at the basis of those two things. In this world we can now begin a little to understand things, and a little to master them by help of science, which has forced its way step by step against the Christian religion, against the churches, and against the opposition of all the old precepts. Science can help us to get over this craven fear in which mankind has lived for so many generations. Science can teach us, and I think our own hearts can teach us, no longer to look around for imaginary supports, no longer to invent allies in the sky, but rather to look to our own efforts here below to make this world a fit place to live in, instead of the sort of place that the churches in all these centuries have made it.[1]

At the practical level of giving a defense or an apology, the task before us is to set forth these statements one at a time, analyze them, put them under the searchlight of truth and coherence, and answer them firmly. The answering must be done in a spirit of deep concern for the objector. The best answer is based on a deep knowledge of the Christian position and its total implication. Instead of promoting fear, Christianity dispels fear. The biblical documents reflect this truth and literally mirror its entire sweeping response to Russell's position with these words: "For God has not given us a spirit of timidity (fear), but of power and love and discipline" (2 Tim. 1:7).

Grounded on the truth that perfect love casts out fear, the Christian simply sorts out the charges of Russell and responds to them. The biblical position on fear includes the radical truth that fear has been generated by man's own turning away from God. In any detailed answer to this position, which would go beyond the limits of this study, there could be a specific delineation of the biblical doctrine of fear. Included would be a forthright invitation to the critic influenced by Russell's position to examine all the evidence.

Responding to Russell again, the apologete can agree that, certainly, many deeds of cruelty and hatred have been done in the name of religion. The issue between naturalism, as espoused by Russell, and biblical Christianity, however, is far deeper than a discussion of what adherents of religion have or have not done. The issue involves defining biblical Christianity. Factual statements can be given in candid response to his ideas. For example, historical evidence abounds to show that true biblical religion in many cases proved to be the fruitful soil and ground for true scientific discovery and scientific achievement.[2] It is a major oversimplification to suggest that science ends fear and has had to function in soil, so to speak, foreign to Christian theism. The depth of commitment to human compassion and understanding that Russell evidenced is indeed commendable. His statements, however, that the churches have made this world an unfit place to live in and that science now is going to undo all the evil done by the churches are far from the truth and must be answered. He has greatly oversimplified the total dimension of the very human struggle and desperation that he sought to remedy.

A "common sense" apologetic, then, can be made by simply taking the statements offered against Christian theism, putting them into a proper framework, and attempting to face the problems. Instances of simple misrepresentation and misunderstanding abound in Russell's famous essay. The examples cited here are sufficient to indicate for any student of apologetics a suggested method for careful response.

Invitation

A final step involves a continuing invitation to the opponent of Christian truth for further discussion and analysis. One might term this a research-and-development phase. Often those bringing objections have never been faced with the prospect of considering the answers to these objections.

There yet remains, however, another area to study. Having gone through the steps for an apologetic method, one could feasibly ask, "How is Christianity really and ultimately vindicated? If all of these arguments and steps in apologetic method are so cogent, then why is there not 'instant validation'?" The next section hopefully can help us evaluate this question of the final vindication of the truth of Christianity against naturalism or other world views. A serious consideration will be made of the Holy Spirit's ministry, which will be seen to be in harmony with the work of argumentation, Christian defense, and evidence.

A PATTERN OF VINDICATION

Introduction

Arguments offered in defense of the faith often involve attesting the truthfulness of Christianity by its trustworthy source, the Word of God. The argumentation simply stated is as follows: God has spoken definitively and freely in His Word, the sacred Scriptures. He Himself has chosen to vindicate and validate His revelation by attesting truth in the process of history. Thus His messengers were empowered to speak His Word, and within that empowerment they acted as agents of God. They were enabled by God to function as His agents in accomplishing His purposes (for example, Moses as God's agent was the leader in a miraculous deliverance of the people of Israel from the hands of their enemies). These events, including the miracle-narratives, were all recorded in Scripture. The miracles openly stand as indications of God's intervention in behalf of His people. They can be studied as recorded, and they invite inquiry and critical analysis.

Another case in point is the supernatural release of Peter from prison as recorded in Acts 12. All the ingredients are here for a balanced interrelationship between what has been called the natural, observable realm of *fact* (chains, prison, soldiers, and gates) and the supernatural, unobservable realm of *faith* (angel, breaking of chains, opening of gates, and release of Peter). The idea that this was a spiritual truth verified by the constant faith of the early church as it records this type of miracle-narrative to bolster its confidence would have been of small comfort to the Roman soldiers who were condemned to death because of their failure to keep a prisoner confined. This recorded event, open to investigation, shows that one cannot separate faith and history with impunity and live in two separate worlds, one of faith, and the other of history and historically verifiable events. The same believers who prayed (a spiritual exercise) observed the physical presence of Peter before them (an observable phenomenon). Luke the physician-historian, trained in the methods of critical discernment and inquiry, records the entire incident. The recorded document is open to verification and study. The conclusion that one is forced to reach is that either this happened exactly the way it was recorded, or it did not. The interpenetration of history and God's action are so close that they cannot be separated. The reverberations of this event were seen in history. The unfolding of the events was recorded and open to investigation. Any fraudulence in the construction of this or other biblical narratives presenting miracles would have compounded the problem for the would-be forger or presenter of falsehood. To be specific, if someone had intended to present this as a story to add credence to the Christian position, he would have had to go to great lengths to carry through the fabrication at all levels. Not only would he have had to invent the miracle-narrative, but he would also have had to invent the narrative in which the after-effects of this case were seen. Thus the account of the repercussions of this also would have had to be manufactured in order to make it look good, so to speak. Then one wonders how far it would have had to go to have the impression of historical validity. It is far better to accept the document at face value, realizing that it has withstood the severest scrutiny and critical analysis during centuries of questioning.

This same kind of conclusion has been cogently demonstrated when the open evidence for the bodily resurrection of the Lord Jesus Christ has been considered.[3]

The kind of evidence surveyed here involves history and biblical events. It is vital that we give a groundwork in apologetics concerning Christianity's claims for truthfulness grounded in just such evidences as miracles. A step-by-step analysis can put the issue before us.

Evidence

Evidence by dictionary definition can be described as "the data on which a judgment or conclusion may be based, or by which proof or probability may be established."[4] One kind of evidence considered earlier was that of the mark of order and symmetry left by the Creator on His creation. This pattern of evidence with its corollary in the cosmological argument was openly presented. Other kinds of equally cogent evidence also can be presented as a challenge to the naturalist, who is in bondage to this universe alone as the entire sphere of reality.

An analogy involving certain types of legal action in court hearings by a judge can possibly help here. Notice that no analogy should be pressed beyond its purpose as a tool for comparison and study. In certain kinds of legal activity, evidence is presented in a hearing to a competent tribunal, a judge, concerning the truthfulness or falsehood of alleged criminal activity. Let us keep this analogy for the sake of comparison. The first step in determining the truth of falsehood of a statement or an action being tested legally is to gather and examine the evidence. In a legal matter a judge seeks to ascertain the validity of the available evidence. In some cases there is even a preliminary hearing, in which a judge listens to evidence and then makes a judgment on the basis of the evidence as to the further adjudication of the case.

By possible analogy and comparison, the naturalist has been presented with the evidence of God's control over history and of God's direct intervention in history in the person of Jesus Christ, His Son. Some of this evidence includes argumentation, such as that given in the form of the cosmological argument. Other forms of this evidence may concern documented cases of fulfilled prophecy in the Bible and the documented case of the bodily resurrection of Jesus Christ from the grave. The analogy of the judge and the person listening to this kind of evidence should not be pressed, however. It holds true only at the level of the actual evidence. The naturalist's rejection of the evidence does not negate the truthfulness of the evidence, but rather demonstrates the obdurateness and close-minded disobedience of the one rejecting it.

Testimony

Testimony is defined as "a declaration or affirmation of fact or truth, such as that given before a court."[5] In a law court a judge not only sifts the evidence presented, but also listens to testimony in the form of oral statements made concerning events and activities under question. There is an analogy here regarding biblical events. Testimony certainly was given, for example, to the event of the resurrection of Christ. This testimony was recorded. The documents are available for evaluation and the testimony is openly offered as an invitation to inquiry and vindication.

Proof

Proof is the effect of evidence. It has been defined as "conclusive demonstration of something."[6] In deciding a legal action a judge listens to evidence and testimony; he then evaluates this material and makes a decision for further action. He states the result of his consideration of the evidence. In some cases this means that he is convinced as to the truthfulness of the situation to which the testimony and evidence point. In other cases, by a process of critical analysis and thinking he decides that the evidence does not lead to proof in this legal sense. Now in reference to Christianity, the objector is the one who is judging the evidence or sifting the testimony; he has already brought reasoned objection against the Christian position. Now, however, the defender asks him or her to look at the evidence and think it through. We believe that the naturalist here, for example, can understand the answers given and has the ability to fit the answers into the focus of the process of thinking out of which the objections were brought.

A judge who is deciding a legal issue may be influenced by many factors. He is trained in legal matters and ideally has a place of responsible leadership; he has demonstrated his ability to discern and analyze evidence and then to draw correct conclusions. Let us say by way of illustration that in a legal inquiry or preliminary hearing the evidence was based on reality—on the actual truth. The testimony corroborated the evidence. The judge, acting according to his training and on the basis of the overwhelming evidence, renders his decision in conformity with truth and proof.

Now here is where the analogy does not follow through. The non-Christian offers objections that need an apology or defense. However, when the non-Christian studies the answer or defense, he or she cannot be likened to the judge in the legal analogy. The reason is that there really is no sure way to predict how the non-Christian will respond to the evidence. Certainly, there will be a natural bias on the part of the non-Christian to turn away from the evidence and to attempt to resist it. In the final validation of the truth claims of Christianity, the Holy Spirit bears an infinite witness to the truthfulness of the entire position. Suppose that the non-Christian has heard the defense, for example, and goes on to believe in the total truth of the gospel (having heard this in the sequence of evangelism/apologetics). Suppose that person accepts the wonderful Good News that rests on the solid foundation of the Christian theistic system. This would verify the fact that the Holy Spirit has been pleased to work in conjunction with, and in interpenetration of, the thinking of the person. The key point here is that the Holy Spirit does not bear witness to propositional error! He, the Spirit of truth, bears witness to the truth.

The distinction made here is valid and is based on a close differentiation between the terms *prove* and *establish*. "*Prove* implies convincing evidence in the form or argument, reasoning, or demonstration. *Establish* adds to *prove* the securing of a position beyond all doubt."[7] The defense of the faith on the grounds of straight thinking about reality, we believe, can *prove* the truthfulness of the Christian position and *defend* Christianity against the charges of naturalism or any other world and life view. Another step is the *establishment* of this position so as to secure obedience to the faith in the gospel proclamation resting on the groundwork of Christian theism. Here it is the work of the Holy Spirit *to establish* the veracity of the evidence in authenticating the Christian position. This delicate balance between proving and establishing is illustrated in Acts 5:32: "And we are witnesses of these things; and *so is* the Holy Spirit, whom God has given to those who obey Him." Among other things, the truth of the resurrection of Jesus Christ is the issue in this verse. This event is a miracle and is part of the groundwork of Christian proclamation, apologetics, and evidence. It is presented boldly as a fact in the same manner in which arguments for the existence of God, reflecting Romans 1:20, are presented as fact. When the non-Christian objector hears the reasoning and evidence, he or she can understand it. Thus, for example, the fact of the Resurrection or of the existence of God can be substantiated or proved to the objector. But the stronger word in this pattern is the term *establish*. Acts 5:32 says the Holy Spirit has been given by God to those who obey Him, i.e., believe and fully trust Him. The Holy Spirit is the infinite Witness to the truth of the existence of God and the resurrection of Christ. God has given the Holy Spirit to those who obey Him by trusting in the Savior as their personal Sin-Bearer and thus in genuine faith claim His forgiveness and cleansing. In this way the truth of the Christian position is *substantiated* or *proved* adequately at the full level of human comprehension. Moreover, it is *established* beyond all shadow of doubt by the witness of the Holy Spirit, who vindicates and validates propositional truth. Thus the truth is both *substantiated* and *established* in the technical sense of these terms.

Calvin's Use of Evidence and Defense

Centuries ago John Calvin urged a proper use of evidence and argumentation in the realm of apologetics. He believed that arguments and answers should be given to objectors, even as has been presented here concerning arguments against naturalism. He felt that these arguments and evidences for the truth of Christianity accomplished something worthwhile. In fact, he chose "Rational Proofs to Establish the Belief of the Scripture" as the title for chapter 8, book 1, of his work *Institutes of the Christian Religion*. In that chapter he wrote:

> There are other reasons, neither few nor weak, for which the dignity and majesty of Scripture are not only affirmed in godly hearts, but brilliantly vindicated against the wiles of its disparagers. . . . Indeed, these human testimonies which exist to confirm it will not be vain if, as secondary aids to our feebleness, they follow that chief and highest testimony.[8]

According to Calvin, therefore, there is on the one hand a pattern for argumentation and for presenting reasons for the dignity and majesty of Scripture as well as for its entire Christian theistic system. This pattern is seen as a secondary aid. This is, to be sure, a subservient but nonetheless valid role. Almost as a preface to this, however, in chapter 7 of the *Institutes,* dealing with the place of the Holy Spirit, he had written:

> For my part, although I do not excel either in great dexterity or eloquence, if I were struggling against the most crafty sort of despisers of God, who seek to appear shrewd and witty in disparaging Scripture, I am confident it would not be difficult for me to silence their clamorous voices. And if it were a useful labor to refute their cavils, I would with no great trouble shatter the boasts they mutter in their lurking places. But even if anyone clears God's Sacred Word from man's evil speaking, he will not at once imprint upon their hearts that certainty which piety requires. . . . Let this point therefore stand: that those whom the Holy Spirit has inwardly taught truly rest upon Scripture, and that Scripture indeed is self-authenticated; . . . we subject our judgment and wit to it as to a thing far beyond any guesswork! This we do, not as persons accustomed to seize upon some unknown thing, which, under closer scrutiny, displeases them, but fully conscious that we hold the unassailable truth![9]

As can be clearly seen here, Calvin balanced the appeal to argumentation and reasoning with the appeal to final validation and vindication of the truth by the Holy Spirit. Notice that he was confident that by stating arguments back to the objectors, he could "silence their clamorous voices." This activity is apologetics—giving answers. Yet Calvin was also equally confident that he would never be able to take the place of the Holy Spirit, who alone would vindicate and establish the truth of the Christian position as set forth in Scripture.

It would seem that modern efforts at reasoning about the Christian faith, stating arguments back to objectors, would function best with the approach that Calvin offered. We can *prove* the truthfulness of Christianity, but we cannot *establish* it, that is, secure its inward acceptance on the part of all objectors. We simply give the statements of response. We then rest our case at that point, always being hopeful as Paul was in his desire to "become all things to all men, that I may by all means save some" (1 Cor. 9:21). In the case of all who have trusted Christ as personal Mediator, Christianity's truth claims are both substantiated and established. The Holy Spirit has established them.

SUMMARY AND CONCLUSION

God the Holy Spirit is the ultimate vindicator. He validates truth as the God of truth. We as Christians therefore know the truthfulness of Christian theism. For the sake of clarity, concern, and commitment to truth, we place reasons and arguments before those who demand a response and who seek answers to the issues of reality. Christians must give answers that assert the objective truth of God's existence. Such an exposure may help open the process of thinking in the mind of the non-Christian so that he or she begins to view the revelation of God as the source of reality.

We believe that apologetics can function in giving answers to the questions raised by opposing systems. Furthermore, the truth of God's existence can be demonstrated through a process of careful thinking. God Himself will certify and establish His truth as He sees fit, in His own way and time and for His greater glory, as contact is made with the many influenced by non-Christian positions.

With this balance of God's action in vindication and the Christian's action in apologetics, there is no violence done to the biblical truth about the witness of the Spirit and the ultimate veracity and validation of Christianity. Argumentation in this context becomes an open avenue of dialogue, consideration, and careful thinking that leads to an open invitation to the critic of Christianity to consider the truth. The limits of apologetics are candidly and openly admitted, and nothing more is expected of defense strategy than simply setting forth the case and speaking to the issue of proving the claims of Christianity.

REVIEW QUESTIONS

1. Summarize each of the four suggested steps in an apologetic method.
2. How can one answer the charge that religion is based almost totally on fear?
3. Concisely define the following words and show how they relate to one another: evidence, testimony, and proof.

4. What is the difference suggested between these two terms: prove and establish? Explain carefully what this means in apologetics.

5. What place did Calvin give to argumentation in answering objectors?

6. What role did Calvin postulate for the Holy Spirit in relation to vindicating and verifying the truth of Christianity?

FOR FURTHER READING

Calvin, John. *Institutes of the Christian Religion*. Translated by Ford Lewis Battles. Library of Christian Classics. Philadelphia: Westminster, 1960. I.1.7–8.

Geisler, Norman L. *Christian Apologetics*. Grand Rapids: Baker, 1976. Chap. 14, pp. 263–83.

Ramm, Bernard. *The Pattern of Authority*. Grand Rapids: Eerdmans, 1959. Chap. 2, pp. 18–45.

_____. *Protestant Christian Evidences*. Chicago: Moody, 1953. Chaps. 4–5, pp. 125–62.

CHAPTER 10

The Problem of History and Christianity

THE PROBLEM STATED

The Facts of History

We know that Christ arose from the dead and is the triumphant conqueror of death. The fact of the Resurrection, like all the other biblical data, stands as truth. Yet a problem arises here for the critic of Christianity. The very definition of the term *fact* causes a lot of concern. What is a fact? How can one be sure something is a fact? Is a fact an event or thing that can be documented in history? If so, how can one be sure that the writer of history did not read more into the events than the actual facts permit? Does all this seem foreign to your way of thinking? Well, it is the type of thinking that historians practice in their desire to get at the sources of truth. The searcher for truth in history faces a veritable battery of tests as he or she pursues this kind of research. In reference to Christianity, non-Christians present reasoned objections to the truth through some process of thinking like the following:

First, the objective historian views anything in history as open to interpretation. The statement that Jesus Christ died, was buried, and rose from the dead is seen as one of probability. In other words it is a statement of history, and the only record of its occurrence appears in books written by people who were committed to the truthfulness of the event. The fact of the Resurrection is seen as standing or falling within a system of interpretation. As far as what really happened in history goes, some students of historical writing feel that reasonable doubt always will be raised about this cardinal truth of Christianity. It is the kind of event, they say, that cannot be repeated. Hence they think the Resurrection does not have the same kind of authenticity that a scientific fact does, for example. Using this type of reasoning the non-Christian declares candidly that Christianity rests on events open to question just as any other events in history are open to question. Furthermore, the non-Christian reasons that history is not like science. Unlike history, it is said, science gives us truth; the scientific method reaches such a high level of verification that a fact of science partakes of much more authenticity than does a fact of history. According to this view, no one can be absolutely sure that a certain event took place on a given day in history. The best that can be offered is a statement of probability. Then the meaning of the fact must be assessed by all the evidence, including documents surrounding the fact and other issues.

Second, the system of interpretation surrounding the fact of Christianity in its assertion of the bodily resurrection of Christ depends for its validity on the assertion of this event. Here again the critic of Christianity is quick to point out that only believers really saw the evidence for the Resurrection; only believers, those already committed to the position, had direct access to the primary data of the case. Indeed, this approach seems to be the gist of a study done by Hugh J. Schonfield in his significant work *The Passover Plot*. [1] Put succinctly, Schonfield has popularized and modernized to some extent an older form of objection to Christian origins that was current in the nineteenth century. Having raised the question of what really happened in history, Schonfield concluded that the entire narrative of the Resurrection was a fabrication. He theorized that it was originated by the Christians as a plot to foster the continued impact and influence of Jesus the Nazarene.

Finally, the implication of this position is that since Christianity is a system of interpretation of reality, it must be seen as an ideology and not as a factual interpretation of life. In other words, as far as the historical fact is concerned, one will never know the truth. The relativity of history is accepted in this view as meaning that there is just not enough evidence to warrant a belief in the absolute truth of the resurrection of Christ. This kind of statement goes beyond historical inquiry, simply because it transcends history; that is, it transcends the realm of data capable of being tested. Ultimately, therefore, in this viewpoint Christianity is seen as moving independently of any historical basis. The ground of Christian certainty, say those who adhere to this position, must be shifted to the subjective data of personal experience.

The Meaning of History

According to this idea of relativity in history, the *meaning* of history becomes more important than the *facts* of history. All facts are seen to fit into a philosophical framework. Usually anything that concerns a claim of activity beyond the natural order will be suspect in this type of thinking. Supernatural events cannot partake of a system of validity. They are incapable of solution and are best left as parts of an interpretive system. With this kind of thinking, then, one is left without having much to do with history but having more to do with interpretation. In addition, the final ground of authority, therefore, can be shifted to human experience and away from sacred Scripture.

THE PROBLEM ANALYZED

Probability Described

The problem of probability now moves to the foreground in this discussion of Christian apologetics. Put simply, many interpreters argue that only the facts of the precise sciences, such as mathematics, can be demonstrated so that there can be no doubt about their authenticity. In such a "hard" science as mathematics, for example, a theorem or sequence of numbers yielding an answer to a problem is demonstrable to the point that there is minimal error or no error at all. Absolute proof is offered, and no questions need to be asked. But the examination of history is said to be another area. When truth is sought in history, it is said that the truth is going to be discerned within the degree of probability that the events took place and that interpretations of events can be offered that make a reasonable pattern of meaning out of the events.

Probability Evaluated

The question of probability must be faced carefully in apologetics. We begin by analyzing the matter, and the following statement helps put the question into proper perspective:

> Truth rests not on possibility nor on plausibility but on Probability. Probability is used here in a strict sense. It means the balance of chances that, given such and such evidence, the event it records happened in a certain way; or, in other cases, that a supposed event did not in fact take place. This balance is not computable in figures as it is in mathematical probability; but it is no less attentively weighed and judged. Judgment is the historian's form of genius, and he himself is judged by the amount of it he can muster. The grounds in which he passes judgment are, again, the common grounds derived from life: general truths, personal and vicarious experience (which includes a knowledge of previous history), and any other kind of special or particular knowledge that proves relevant.[2]

Seen in this light, the term *probability* is not viewed with mistrust by defenders of the Christian faith. However, when viewed in another light, the term might pose an immediate problem to believers. It might seem that if probability is admitted into the defense in matters such as the historical fact of the Resurrection, then there is seemingly an implicit willingness to deny the integrity of the witnesses and to say that maybe the event did not happen after all! Since there can be no uncertain sound in the giving of clear defense, it does appear at first glance that the Christian defender who knows that the Resurrection is a fact surrenders needless ground by saying that probability will function here.

In evaluating this in more detail, however, I believe that the apologete can make a Christian defense very ably here, neither abandoning the concept of probability nor compromising the truth of Scripture. It appears that the probability concept will function in the common ground that exists between the Christian and the non-Christian. In the common ground of communication, where the Christian and the non-Christian are dealing with documents, written records, and testimony, the Christian can offer an open invitation to the critic to examine the credentials of Christianity. The historical documents of Scripture deal with concrete data—hard evidence, so to speak—that can be verified and tested for credibility. This is *not* to say that we subject Scripture to human reason, but we are saying that we *invite* human reasoning to investigate the open and clear factual basis of the faith. Regarding the common tasks of witness and defense, I have attempted to maintain a clear distinction between the two. In 1 Corinthians 9:19–23, Paul gives us a biblical principle that can help. Paul stated at the conclusion of that passage: "I have become all things to all men, that I may by all means save some." Paul did not imply here that he denied the gracious action of God in the communication of saving truth to people. Rather, both the context of the verse and the immediate teaching indicate that Paul was willing to identify himself in some measure with attitudes, concepts, and patterns of thinking held by non-Christians. Paul would do this to the extent that there was no compromise of truth involved and to the extent that he was concerned that individuals should see the truth of the gospel. Thus 1 Corinthians 9:22b in particular has a primary value in its interpretation concerning the matter of presenting the truth of the gospel, that is, the Christian witness or evangelistic message.

By application, Paul's willingness to become all things to all people could be seen as allowing plenty of involvement with non-Christians in the arenas of thoughtful analysis, discussion, and willing argumentation. It appears that the Christian defender, on the common ground of communication, can openly enter the so-called arena of *probability* with the idea of being all things to all people. By this we mean it is not wrong for the apologete to allow the documents of Scripture to be investigated and studied in the light of methods of dealing with testimony and evidence and to move in the same orbit of probability as defined earlier. If the apologete does not adopt such a stance, he or she may seem to communicate at the very level of contact with individuals who need an answer to their objections a spirit of unwillingness to open the door to inquiry. On the ground of the certainty of the event, let us say of the Resurrection, the defender of the faith has both a subjective certitude and an objective certainty that the event took place. How can its factuality be vindicated? One way is on the ground of its validation in keeping with the tests of the historical validity.

Historical Validity Tested

It is interesting to notice in connection with this discussion that many professional historians tentatively accept evidence, believing that facts can be documented and verified. Louis Gottschalk, a former professor of history at the University of Chicago, put together a representative work entitled *Understanding History*. Gottschalk sets forth some readily applicable guides to a search for truth in the realm of probability that are worthy of the attention of Christian defenders. He comments on the tests as follows:

> The historian, however, is prosecutor, attorney for the defense, judge, and jury all in one. But as judge he rules out no evidence whatever if it is relevant. To him any single detail of testimony is credible— even if it is contained in a document obtained by force or fraud, or is otherwise impeachable, or is based on hearsay evidence, or is from an interested witness—provided it can pass four tests.[3]

This is crucial for our discussion. The believer presents the evidence for the factual basis of Christianity. This evidence is contained in documents from "interested witnesses." The Christian need not compromise the faith, indeed must not compromise the faith in defending it. But the Christian defender does not ask the non-Christian objector to accept the fact without first contemplating the entire fabric of evidence that our sovereign God chose to integrate with the fact. If the non-Christian were asked to accept the interpretive system first in order to know the truthfulness of the facts later, the implication would be that there are two different kinds of processes for knowing data. One process deals with presupposition, while the other deals with fact. It is vitally and even dynamically true that the fact of the Resurrection stands on an entire system, and its meaning is never understood apart from that system. Notice that its *meaning* is never understood apart from the system of Christian truth. However, its *actuality*, its *verifiability*, and its *truth* stand whether anyone ever understands or accepts the system that unfolds its meaning! One way of verifying its truthfulness is the open investigation of the evidence. This open investigation does not necessarily mean that the Christian expects the critic, who brings objections to supernatural events such as the Resurrection, to *believe the evidence;* but the Christian does expect that the *evidence is believable* and verifiable.

Gottschalk's work can serve as a feasible guide for verifiability. Let us first summarize his four tests and then study them:

1. *The test of ability.* Was the source of the account of an event, the primary witness, *able* to tell the truth?

2. *The test of attitude.* Was the source or primary witness manifesting a willingness, or an attitude commensurate with willingness, to tell the truth?

3. *The test of accuracy.* Was the primary witness accurate in stating the truth?

4. *The test of authority or attestation.* Is there any other attesting source or are there other attesting sources to give independent corroboration of the information under examination?

After offering these principles. Gottschalk concludes: "Any detail (regardless of what the source or who the author) that passes *all four* tests is credible historical evidence."[4]

THE PROBLEM SOLVED

Introduction

The apologetic significance of Gottschalk's work cannot be denied. The historical biblical account of Christ's resurrection openly invites inquiry and investigation. For example, there is the documented statement of His ability after the Resurrection to take food (an entity subject to measurement, weight, test for substance, and so forth) into a body that transcends spatial limitations. Crucial to the discussion, then, is this question: Did this really *happen?* Christian classicist and veteran historian E. M. Blaiklock puts the issue clearly for the Christian and the non-Christian alike:

> The trial and death of Jesus are better documented than most other events in ancient history. The events which follow the trial and death can similarly be submitted to the historian's scrutiny. They are so far from being remote from his inquiry, that it is the task of every Christian historian, indeed of every Christian, to examine and assess their truth and their significance. Destroy the historical basis for such happenings, and the faith is simultaneously destroyed. The firm rooting of the Christian faith in history was the potent element which ensured its victory over Mithraism, its doughtiest opponent, a cult which rested on a clutter of myth. The Christians did not "find it necessary" to build a joyful proclamation on a rapidly devised substructure of myth, and

thereby ensure their rejection by the world, their persecution, and frequent martyrdom. Conclusions of a theological nature based by the New Testament writers on the empty tomb of their conviction, may be outside the scope of historical inquiry, but if Peter actually "saw the linen clothes lying, and the cloth which had been about His head folded up apart", if the same fisherman actually walked with the risen Jesus on the beach near Capernaum, his further statement: "This Jesus God raised up", can be allowed to follow without the lamentably vague assertion that 'Peter has drawn upon the medium of myth to affirm the faith into which he had been led'.[5]

The need to be selective requires that we look at some of the tension areas in Christian apologetics. Christ's resurrection most assuredly is one of them. The Christian defender states that the Resurrection itself, according to the entire pattern of its meaning as set forth in the biblical evidence, is a verification and vindication of the fact that God has accomplished something in history. The avenues of the Christian theistic system, including God's existence, revelation, purpose in history, redemptive plan for mankind, and victory in history, all converge on the stupendous event of the bodily resurrection of Jesus from the grave, as He Himself had promised. Jesus had interpreted the meaning of the Resurrection, and meaning and interpretation are inextricably interwoven in this massive event. Since the Ressurection is a part of the warp and woof of history, it can be classified as something able to be tested and evaluated.

Verification

The Test of ability. The tests we referred to earlier apply here. With the biblical accounts of the Resurrection before us, it is easy to go through the evidence step by step with the tests of credibility in mind. Our investigation here is not an attempt to subject the documents to criticism or doubt, but rather our purpose is to engage in a disciplined inquiry. The purpose of the first test is to determine the ability of the witness to tell the truth.

Competency and ability to tell the truth function at several levels. They refer to the ability of the witness to observe, record, and recall accurately what happened. Several factors affect the observer's ability: health, general education and training, skill in accurate recording, and so forth. Without unduly belaboring the issue, it needs to be pointed out that Christian apologetes have often demonstrated that the fact of the Resurrection easily stands at this test level, for the ability of the witnesses has been verified.[6] The varied lines of evidence in the biblical narratives as recorded by Matthew, Mark, Luke, and John permit a wide range of testing. Matthew, for example, was trained in observation. It is apparent that he was able to weigh evidence, for he was a person with obvious accounting skills used in assessing property valuation for tax purposes. The impelling truth is that the witnesses to the evidence of the Resurrection were predisposed at first to reject the evidence! In other words, their framework of thinking—one could even say their presuppositional basis, or their presuppositions—was set in a framework that would not initially accept the evidence. Amazingly, therefore, it was the gradual realization of the truth of the evidence that changed their entire framework or presuppositional way of looking at the fact.

Sometimes it is asserted that presuppositions control the facts, a person's coming to evidence, and even the meaning of the facts. A more coherent understanding of the significance of Christ's resurrection would appear to include the realization that there is a sharp difference between the *knowledge* of truth and the *acceptance* of truth. Thus the truth that Christ arose from the dead can be *known*, verified, and examined at the identical level of investigation where observation, recording data, and probability function. The demonstrable nature of the Resurrection was so massive and so irrefutable that it virtually staggered the presuppositions of the first observers. They were predisposed against believing it. This is hardly the example of a "framework" or presuppositional shift first, then an acceptance of evidence on the ground of a brand new framework. Rather, they accepted the evidence first and then believed, or changed their framework. In the early chapters of Acts Peter is revealed as a believer whose life was dramatically changed because he accepted the fact of Christ's resurrection. He obviously did not leap to this conclusion by first stating, "I have projected myself into the reasonable framework of the angelic heralds who confidently assert that this Jesus is not dead, but is risen. I have taken by faith the presuppositional framework of the women who first reported this and who apparently really believed it, and now, too, I can confidently approach this fact of the Resurrection on the solid presuppositional framework of my newfound faith in the God who raised Jesus." Peter *did not* go through any such arduous or even theoretical kind of "ideological" shift. He was simply overpowered by the evidence and believed.

The test of ability applied to the apostolic witnesses of the Resurrection and to the individuals who recorded the evidence in the gospels forms a fitting area for vindicating the truth of the Resurrection. At each step of the way—beginning with the observation of the evidence and going on to reflect on the event to recall the surrounding incidents, and, finally, to record the event—the apostles manifested exactly the kind of transparent honesty and candor that is expected of good witnesses. The documents are open for all to study. The competence of the writers and their commitment to candor and truthfulness are openly verifiable.

The test of attitude. Put simply, this test approaches the documents that record the Resurrection and asks, Were the witnesses willing to tell the truth? Were their demeanor and attitude such that they did not deliberately tell falsehoods or twist the truth? Historians caution that we must discern carefully in the matter of studying the statements and witness of someone who may benefit from distorting the truth or someone who is bent on simply putting out propaganda rather than truth.

To be sure, the early Christian witnesses to the evidence of the Resurrection might be charged with having a conspiracy or a plot to propagate a falsehood in order to manifest a coherence and unity with what Jesus had said. They might be charged with wanting to add credence to a false position in order to perpetuate the ideals and teachings of Jesus. Here again the Christian defender can invite the objector to practice the same kind of reasoning and thinking he or she would use in reaching decisions about any issue of fact. The early Christian message developed and flourished in the face of bitter opposition. The opposition spokesmen knew the facts of the life of Jesus. The silent, penetrating evidence of the empty tomb was never adequately answered by any of the sharpest critics of the Christian message. The entire fabric of actions surrounding the historical basis for the Christian faith was at all times and at all levels open to public inquiry and investigation. The apostles were not propagandists but proclaimers. What they proclaimed has the ring of truth. Furthermore, their message was never challenged with respect to accuracy. The most astute critics never produced verifiable or testable evidence to deny the truth of the Resurrection. A careful reading of the preface to Luke's gospel (1:1–4), for example, reveals a passage that moves solidly in the framework of Greek classicism; the words are those of a person who had discernment and who was bent on setting forth truth, not propaganda.

The test of accuracy. This test provides a ground for evaluating the credibility of the witnesses to the Resurrection. We will limit it primarily to the documents themselves as the recorded and authoritative account of the witnesses. These documents are the four Gospels, as well as the biblical record of the apostolic preaching and references to the core of the apostolic teaching in the New Testament. A candid reading of the Resurrection narratives in the Gospels will reveal the striking phenomenon that the aura of truth pervades throughout. This is apparent when one considers that the accounts stand with no editing. No mastermind attempts to iron out all apparent variations, and no attempt is made to force each writer into a wooden and artificial pattern of writing. In other words, if the Christian position had really been a carefully designed plot, the first thing an astute schemer or group of schemers would have done would have been to get the story straight, so to speak. They would most assuredly have masterminded their narratives so that they had a well-established format, and no apparent discrepancies. Now, certainly, someone can argue that forgers, or purveyors of falsehood, could have lent an air of authenticity to the accounts by allowing them to stand with variations. But such reasoning goes too far into the unknown and into meaningless speculation and supposition. Suffice it to say that the contemporaries of the Christian believers in the first century had adequate time to go out and survey the evidence and to attempt to produce a crushing answer to the Christian faith. They had adequate force, the Roman world power was available, and any plot to deceive the multitudes would most assuredly have been discovered sooner or later. Certainly, the stupendous claims made by these early Christians as to the miraculous ground in history on which the faith was built would make the rejection of them with a factual basis all the more crucial to the critics of the faith. All in all, this avenue of verification takes its place as another example of the reliability of the Christian position.

The test of attestation. Historians are concerned in evaluating the credibility of a witness to know if there are other sources that can give independent corroboration or attestation to the statements of the witness. Again, this raises a good area for consideration of the credibility of the Christian position. Each of the Gospel narratives could ultimately qualify as an independent source, thus meeting one specification for corroboration. The reliability of the New Testament documents has been ably and carefully defined and defended.[7] Furthermore, secular historical references to Jesus also have been very thoroughly documented.[8]

Only one issue demands attention here. The first-century Jewish historian Flavius Josephus (c. A.D. 37–103) gives corroborative evidence of the details of history, including a reference to the claims of Christians about the bodily resurrection of Jesus. The citation from Josephus has been challenged. Some feel that Christians might have been involved in tampering with the documentation to the point of inserting the reference to Christ. The charge, of course, needs to be examined openly and sanely. The quotation in full is as follows:

> Now there was about this time Jesus, a wise man, if it be lawful to call him a man, for he was a doer of wonderful works, a teacher of such men as received the truth with pleasure. He drew over to him both many of the Jews, and many of the Gentiles. He was the Christ, and when Pilate, at the suggestion of the principal men among us, had condemned him to the cross, those that loved him at the first did not forsake him; for he appeared to them alive again the third day; as the divine prophets had foretold these and ten thousand other wonderful things concerning him. And the tribe of Christians so named from him are not extinct at this day.[9]

The debate about the accuracy of Josephus here has been lively and will doubtless continue. One thing is quite clear: the portrait of Josephus as the major source of Jewish history between 100 B.C. and A.D. 100 is untainted and unmarred by criticism. Certain allowances are always made for bias and error. Again, functioning along the

lines of studying the conditions favorable to credibility, one principle that guides historians is the concept that when a reference or
statement is prejudicial to a witness, that is, would seem to go
against the beliefs or positions of the witness, it certainly gains
credibility and accuracy.[10] Most assuredly, the position of Josephus
as a Jew has not benefited by his testimony as to the evidence of
Jesus' resurrection!

A studied consensus would seem to be that this quotation is
accurate and represents the original work by Josephus. R. C. Stone's
helpful summary gives a balanced viewpoint here:

> Recent archeological discoveries at Qumran and Masada have indicated
> that the account of Josephus is remarkably accurate and ranks him high
> as a topographer. The student of the NT has in Josephus a wealth of
> material on agriculture, industry, religion, politics, and the outstanding
> personalities of Gospel history: Herod, Pilate, the two Agrippas, Felix,
> and others. As a historian many have distrusted him, mostly because
> they disapprove of him as a traitor. He is no more affected by human
> error (of memory, faulty sources, bias, and the like) than others of his
> time. The passage concerning Jesus (*Antiquities* XVIII, 63ff.) has been
> regarded by some as a Christian interpolation; but the bulk of evidence,
> both external and internal, marks it as genuine. Josephus must have
> known the main facts about the life and death of Jesus, and his histo-
> rian's curiosity certainly would lead him to investigate the movement
> which was gaining adherents even in high circles. Arnold Toynbee
> rates him among the five greatest Hellenic historians, along with
> Herodotus, Thucydides, Xenophon, and Polybius.[11]

Josephus seems a fitting source for the corroboration of the testimony of the biblical writers. If accepted as a genuine source, the
quotation corroborates the claim that there was evidence that Jesus
arose from the grave. The probability that it is accurate is high. If this
is rejected, we still have the corroboration of the independent Gospel
narratives, plus the widely circulated apostolic preaching as reported
in the New Testament. Notice the apologetic significance of this,
however. We are *not* resting the truthfulness of the Resurrection on
the principle of probability. We are resting the verification and validation of the evidence on this principle for the sake of open discussion of an event that is established as true on the ground of the Word
of God.

Conclusion

The Christian has nothing to fear from truth. The tests for truthfulness serve as avenues of verification of the truth. Christian defenders are keenly aware that there is a difference between *knowledge* of truth and *acceptance* of truth. On these grounds we have argued for the dependability of the historical method of research and for the accuracy of the function of probability in this research. Furthermore, the question of science versus history is one of many facets. Some would rule out history as participating in the same degree of accuracy as science or mathematics. It is interesting to test this kind of thinking in the face of the rise of the science of archaeology. The development of this science itself has established the accuracy of such things as pottery chronology. Now, archaeology is not like mathematics or chemistry. There is no way that the data of archaeology can be subjected to this kind of test: repeatability will guarantee testability and accuracy. Yet on the strict grounds of scientific objectivity, archaeologists, as scientists, can take a fragment of pottery and by scientific analysis date that fragment historically with a very high degree of accuracy. The point here is that no one need question the accuracy of statements open to historical verification on the grounds that these are not "scientific" or "capable of scientific validation."

The fact and meaning of the Resurrection are openly verifiable, for the evidence can be examined. That the Resurrection is true can be demonstrated. It is established by the work of the Holy Spirit, as expressed in the illustration of Acts 5:32. The case for Christianity and the work of apologetics rest with the historical verification of this fact. Some will certainly never accept its truth. Their lack of acceptance does not invalidate it any more than the believer's acceptance validates it. The fact and its meaning stand on the ground of Scripture. The Christian defense has accomplished its purpose when the evidence is presented and when the objector is invited to examine the evidence.

REVIEW QUESTIONS

1. Why do some students of history feel that reasonable doubt always will be raised about the historical truth or fact of the resurrection of Jesus Christ?

2. What suggested contrast is made here between science and history?

3. If relativity in history is accepted, what is the implication of this for Christianity?

4. What specifically is the meaning of the term *probability?*

5. How can the Christian defender enter the so-called arena of probability without casting doubt on the historical nature of the great truths on which Christianity rests?

6. What is the test of ability and how, briefly, does the fact of the resurrection of Christ stand with reference to this test?

7. With respect to the response of Peter to the Resurrection, which came first: a shift or change in presuppositions, or an acceptance of evidence?

8. What is the test of attitude?

9. What is the test of accuracy?

10. What is the test of attestation?

11. Josephus has been questioned as a valid corroboration of the Resurrection. What can be said positively about Josephus as a historian?

FOR FURTHER READING

Blaiklock, E. M. *A Layman's Answer.* Valley Forge, Pa.: Judson, 1970. Chaps. 2–6, pp. 26–81.

Geisler, Norman L. *Christian Apologetics.* Grand Rapids: Baker, 1976. Chaps. 15–16, pp. 285–327.

Montgomery, John Warwick. *History and Christianity.* Downers Grove, Ill.: InterVarsity, 1971.

_____. *The Shape of the Past.* Rev. ed. Minneapolis: Bethany, 1975. All of this is helpful. Note especially essay no. 8, pp. 375–82, in part 2: "History: Public or Private? A Defense of John Warwick Montgomery's Philosophy of History" by Paul Feinberg.

_____. *Faith Founded on Fact.* Nashville: Thomas Nelson, 1978.

CHAPTER 11

Some Challenges
Concerning Christ

We have responded to challenges against the truthfulness of Christian theism in regard to the existence of God and the historical validity of Christianity. We now will consider challenges to the truth about Jesus Christ that have persisted over the centuries. This chapter will necessarily be selective, for certainly there are many more facets of Christology (the study of truth about Christ) than can possibly be covered in the present book. Three vital areas must be dealt with. First, we will consider challenges relating to Christ's entrance into human history—His miraculous conception and the Virgin Birth. Second, we will respond to a unique attack on Christianity that alleges that the Dead Sea Scrolls throw specific light on the early years of Jesus. Finally, we will deal briefly with a theory that attempts to trace the origin of the Resurrection narratives to the pagan mystery religions.

THE VIRGIN BIRTH OF CHRIST

The position of biblical Christianity here is clearly stated in Scripture. The statements in the text of Matthew 1:16–25 and Luke 1:26–37 categorically detail the truth of the miraculous conception and virgin birth of Christ.

The Challenge Stated

The arguments against Christ's virgin birth have been articulated for centuries. In recent years these arguments have been focalized by a Jewish scholar and writer, Hugh J. Schonfield, in his work entitled *The Passover Plot*. Lest the reader miss the bluntness and force of this attack against Christianity, here are the author's own words on this subject:

> There was nothing peculiar about the birth of Jesus. He was not God incarnate and no Virgin Mother bore him. The Church in its ancient zeal fathered a myth and became bound to it as dogma. Since Christians largely continue to suppose that their faith stands or falls by the doctrine of the deity of Christ the dogma goes on being sustained to the detriment of what is really significant about the person and contribution of Jesus.[1]

Schonfield implies in his book that the early church deliberately fabricated the narrative of the virgin birth of Christ. He thinks the church did this in an attempt to add a dimension of the miraculous to Jesus and to deify Jesus the man. Schonfield states:

> This teaching became overlaid in Gentile-Christianity by the concept of the Incarnation, which asserted in pagan fashion that Jesus had been born Son of God by a spiritual act of fatherhood on God's part which fertilized the womb of the Virgin Mary, and then went on to claim by an elaboration and partial misunderstanding of Pauline theology that the Son of God had eternally pre-existed and was manifested on earth in Jesus, who thus from birth was God dwelling in a human body by a hypostatic union of the two natures.[2]

The Challenge Answered

The Christian answer to such charges has been voluminous and carefully prepared for centuries. One avenue of cogent response has been to question the entire process of developing a myth of this proportion, for that is what is implied in the attack. The implication is that the theological expression of the Virgin Birth came from sources other than the Hebrew tradition, such as Gentile or pagan. The time necessary to develop and articulate such a legend is blithely overlooked by those who attack the origins of Christianity in this way. Robert Gromacki carefully sifts through the charges and concludes:

> The authors traced Christ's human beginning back to the virgin birth because that is exactly what happened. Three of the four Gospels were written within thirty years of Christ's earthly life. Many who had ob-

served His ministry were still alive at the time of their composition. No myth or legend would have been able to permeate the church in that short period of time. If the early church had recognized in the narratives of Matthew or Luke mythological influence, they would have detected and rejected it.[3]

The evidence from the Gospel of Matthew alone dispels the conjecture of Schonfield. Matthew, a Jew, was carefully trained in record keeping, for he was a tax expert in his Roman-dominated homeland. His careful recording of the narrative of Christ's birth is devoid of any shred of evidence that would link it with Gentile sources. Of course, a critic would have to assume that Matthew or some editor came into contact with the Gentile mythological-origin theory of Jesus' birth quite early and simply inserted this adaptation of that background into the record here. However, such a conjecture cannot stand the scrutiny of hard analysis, especially in the light of the theological purposes of Matthew and his careful and accurate presentation of Jesus as the Descendant of David and of Abraham.

Also, the record of history after the close of the apostolic age has been neglected by Schonfield in his attack on the origin of Christianity through his rejection of the true nature of Christ's entrance into history. Thomas Boslooper explains that there is no valid basis in history for a pagan origin of the account of the Virgin Birth. He states:

> Contemporary writers invariably use only secondary sources to verify such claims. The scholars whose judgment they accept rarely produced or quoted the primary sources. The literature of the old German *religionsgeschichtliche Schule*, which produced this conclusion and which has become the authority for contemporary scholars who wish to perpetuate the notion that the virgin birth in the New Testament has a non-Christian source, is characterized by brief word, phrase, and sentence quotations that have been lifted out of context or incorrectly translated and used to support preconceived theories. Sweeping generalizations based on questionable evidence have become dogmatic conclusions that cannot be substantiated on the basis of careful investigation.[4]

An analysis of the pagan accounts of unusual births and of the biblical account of the virgin birth of Christ reveals striking dissimilarities and refutes the charge that Schonfield brought. First, with respect to the background of such legends as the divine birth of Perseus, for example, there is no solid historical basis for this legend; there is no viable contact with events in time-space history. By contrast, the biblical account of Christ's virgin birth is linked inextricably into the fabric of time-space history, and the account appears in documents that can themselves be tested and vindicated in the historical arena.

Second, the contrast between pagan mythology and Christian theology on the distinctions as to the one born is definitive. The progeny in these mythological accounts is usually seen as half-deity and half-human. Furthermore, in these myths or legends, the child born came into being as a substantive entity and was not seen as preexistent. In contrast, the biblical accounts refer to the eternal Second Person of the Godhead, who always existed and hence did not begin to exist through the event of the Virgin Birth, and Scripture preserves the perfect balance of deity and humanity. Thus, for example, Paul's teaching about Christ's preexistence is clearly and carefully enunciated in Philippians 2:6–7: "Who, although He existed [which can as well read, *although He continued existing*] in the form of God, did not regard equality with God a thing to be grasped, but emptied Himself, taking the form of a bond-servant."

Third, the contrast between pagan or non-Christian accounts of unusual births and the narratives of the Virgin Birth in the Bible is apparent in the actual wording and content. Often ludicrous and debasing sensuality is seen in the pagan accounts, whereas the sober and striking realism of the biblical accounts, with their simplicity and dignity, is easily observable.

Fourth, the difference can be clearly seen between pagan accounts and Scripture as to the condition or development of the one who is born. One observes an unreal anachronism persisting in pagan accounts. For example, in the account of the birth of Pallas Athena, "who had no mother, he sprang out of the head of Zeus, full grown and in full armor."[5] There is no such unreal anachronism present in the account of Christ's coming to earth. Historian-physician Luke, within the strict guidelines of his careful research, records the words of Elizabeth in her greeting of Mary prior to Jesus' birth. The Lucan narrative states the balance of deity and humanity with this careful and accurate wording: "Blessed among women *are* you, and blessed is the *fruit of your womb!* [genuine humanity] And how has it *happened* to me, that the *mother of my Lord* [genuine deity] should come to me?" (Luke 1:42–43, italics mine). A real and normal human development is portrayed in Luke 2:52: "And Jesus kept increasing in wisdom and stature, and in favor with God and men."

Summarizing these contrasts, Gromacki carefully notes:

> The differences between the pagan and the Gospel accounts are so great that no one can demonstrate that the Biblical authors either borrowed from the mythological sources or refined them. Just because the pagan accounts were written first doesn't mean that the Gospel writers copied them. This is a perfect example of the logical fallacy *post hoc ergo propter hoc* ["after this, therefore, because of this"]. Plato wrote about the existence of God long before Paul authored his epistles, but the latter was in no way dependent upon the Greek philosopher.[6]

THE EARLY YEARS OF JESUS

The Problem

Some who reject the truth of biblical Trinitarianism have attempted to question the uniqueness and authority of Christ by an unusual method of interpreting the evidence of the Dead Sea Scrolls. For clarification, we should at the outset note that this is not a majority interpretation offered by scholars who have worked with the Scrolls. But the kind of charges that must be answered here work their way into the popular level, and most probably it is at this level that our defense will be made, anyway, in the great issues of apologetics.

The problem, simply stated, is one of interpreting the meaning of the Dead Sea Scrolls as to the origins of the Christian faith. Popular charges or claims have been dramatically made in books that readers by the thousands have consulted. An example of such a book is Charles Francis Potter's *Lost Years of Jesus Revealed*. The claims in Potter's book must be answered.

The gist of Potter's popularly written theory is that Jesus was influenced by a group of cultic Jews living at Qumran, the community on the shores of the Dead Sea where ascetic life was coupled with apparently rigorous scribal work in copying Scripture and in

writing commentaries and other data. The implications of this kind
of reasoning followed by Potter would be to deny the unique origin
of the teaching of Christ, as well as the supernatural in His total
ministry. Instead of being the God-man who lived in the perfect
balance of genuine deity and genuine humanity as recorded in the
New Testament documents, Jesus becomes in this view a human
being who spent some early years of his life at that very community
of Qumran. Potter's view is that Jesus' teaching about life, God,
messianic ideals, and other areas was virtually shaped or certainly
influenced by the teachings of this cult.

An example of Potter's thinking on this subject follows:

> When the Qumran manuscripts are properly recognized and evalu-
> ated in relation to the books of our very much edited and expurgated
> New Testament, the doctrine of the Holy Spirit will have to go, and will
> take with it the doctrine of the Trinity, which never was in the New
> Testament anyway.[7]

The reason for this charge brought by Potter lies in his interpretation of the evidence in the Dead Sea Scrolls. One of the books studied
by Potter in the Scrolls collection is entitled the Manual of Discipline,
which gives detailed teaching about water baptism as the initiatory
rite into the group. From the teachings enunciated in conjunction with
baptism, Potter has concluded that the term "Spirit of truth" was
expanded and changed by Christians into an actual personification of
truth, or into a veritable person of the Godhead known as the Holy
Spirit. Potter thus believes that this doctrine was an invention of the
early Christans, not a pure teaching of Jesus, the Founder of Christianity. Many scholars believe that this group of people living at
Qumran were Essenes. The inferential type of argumentation that
Potter uses moves along the following line: Since Jesus did not openly
condemn the Essenes, and since some elements of His teaching are
similar to elements found in this literature, then Jesus really is not the
unique and only begotten Son of God. Rather, Jesus was a man, a
powerful teacher who drank freely of the ideas of the Essenes. Having
perhaps spent some time at this community of Qumran, he returned to
the world of his day to proclaim true righteousness and to identify
himself with the messianic ideals of his people.

Put succinctly, the position of Potter means that Christianity evolved gradually as a religion and as a teaching from some specific original strands of Essene thought. Potter states:

> The Holy Spirit, or Holy Ghost, evidently grew out of the early church's gradual build-up into a vague personal metaphysical spirit, nebulous but powerful, from Jesus' frequent references (according to the Fourth Gospel) to the Spirit of Truth which would guide his disciples into all the truth.
>
> Jesus' "Spirit of Truth" phrase and idea most probably reflects the Essene "Holy Spirit of Truth" referred to in their Manual of Discipline . . . which was certainly very different from the later Christian Holy Spirit, the third Person of the Trinity.[8]

The implications here for biblical Christianity are obvious. Under the general framework of searching for truth, Potter feels that he is leading people into the light of rational truth by exposing what he believes to be the mythological foundation of Christianity. Thus the gist of his argument is that Jesus spent some years of His life at Qumran as a student at that cultural oasis. There is a suggestion here from Potter that perhaps Jesus developed many of His teachings from those of an individual in the records of the Qumran group called the Teacher of Righteousness, who had evidently been executed nearly a century before Jesus' time.

The Response

In answering Potter the Christian defender can point out that his position rests largely on an argument from silence and a great amount of inference. There is no historical evidence that Jesus contacted the Qumran cultists. Certainly, there is nothing wrong with implying that Jesus knew of the group. However, the environment of Jesus at crucial points in the biblical narrative is different from that of Essenism. For example, His early training, His avowed determination to establish His teaching authority in the temple, and His entire framework of thinking and teaching do not partake of the Essene tradition. Christian scholars working with the evidence have answered claims of any suggested ideological links between Jesus and Essenism. Several important contrasts emerge.

First, the Qumran community adherents built a strict legalistic way of life. This is obvious to any reader of such a writing as The

Zadokite Document. A long list of instructions for the Sabbath can be seen in this literature. Here are some specific examples of this legalistic concept:

> No one is to eat on the Sabbath day anything that has not been prepared in advance. He is not to eat anything that happens to be lying about in the field, neither is he to drink of anything that was not previously in the camp. . . . No one is to wear soiled clothes or clothes that have been put in storage unless they first be laundered and rubbed with frankincense. . . . No one is to raise his hand to strike it with his fist. . . . No one is to take anything out of his house, or bring anything in from outside. . . . No one is to pick up rock or dust in a dwelling place.[9]

In striking contrast to this, Jesus set Himself before His hearers as one who acted authoritatively, even when His actions clashed with Jewish interpretations. Jesus' words in Mark 2:27 stand as a clear refutation of the claim that His teachings could have links with Essenism of the type manifested in the citations above. After sanctioning the action of the disciples in harvesting grain as they walked through the fields on the Sabbath, Jesus pointedly said, "The Sabbath was made for man, and not man for the Sabbath. Consequently, the Son of Man is Lord even of the Sabbath" (Mark 2:27–28).

Second, the Essenes were a deeply ascetic group. Entire sections of the Manual of Discipline are devoted to strict rules governing the community. Contrary to this, Jesus certainly was not an ascetic. The charge brought against Him in Matthew 11:19 reveals that He was a friend of tax-gatherers and sinners. His every move was watched by His critics.

Third, ritual lustrations and ceremonial baths were vital to Essene action and life at Qumran. This is reflected by the determined efforts at water preservation that can be demonstrated to have occurred at Qumran, a normally arid region. These ceremonial washings or baths included those taken before dining. This seems to indicate a rather meticulous attitude to ceremonial purity with a stress on externals. Jesus, in contrast, pointed out the far greater problem of inward impurity and the need for inward cleansing when He said, "Not what enters into the mouth defiles the man, but what proceeds out of the mouth, this defiles the man" (Matt. 15:11).

Fourth, Jesus placed great stress on the temple at Jerusalem. He taught often in the temple. Indeed, during His last days of ministry, He chose the temple as the scene of teaching and messianic works, even challenging the very core of Judaism with His actions. By way of contrast, the Essenes were not totally in sympathy with the central place of the temple. They most certainly did not sacrifice animals, and they were separated from mainstream Judaism on the ground that they were cut off from temple sacrifices.

Fifth, apparently the Essenes and cultists of Qumran rejected bodily resurrection.[10] With dualism inherent in their outlook, they apparently could not harmonize the idea of a pure spirit being reunited with a body that partook of material substance, and thus evil. The New Testament documents show, in contrast again, Jesus' teaching concerning His own resurrection (Mark 8:31), and His interpretation of the event.

In conclusion, one finds contrasts that are far-reaching and definitive between the teachings of Jesus and the later apostles and the teachings of Essenism and the Qumran community. There is no proof that establishes any link between Jesus and Qumran.

Then what about the Dead Sea Scrolls and the Christian faith? Charles F. Potter certainly believes that the Scrolls more plausibly reveal the origin of Jesus by linking His teaching to that of Qumran. Potter thinks Jesus' early so-called silent years were spent living right at that place by the Dead Sea. He states:

> For, in the light of these Scrolls, their contents and particularly their pre-Christian origin, there must take place a radical and thorough review, restudy, and revaluation of extremely important matters such as the education, beliefs, parentage, deity, and even the existence of the unusual person named Jesus, called Christ, together with the related problems of the origin, founders, liturgy, doctrines, and early literature of the Christian Church. . . . The radical reconsideration of all these important ideas and doctrines in the light of the Scrolls is our duty in spite of the opposition of vested theological interests and institutions, whose representatives apparently are already trying desperately to conceal or at least minimize the importance of the manuscripts.[11]

This is erroneous. Millar Burrows, eminent clergyman and scholar, provides a fitting answer to the conclusions of Potter. He wrote his first edition of a scholarly work on the Dead Sea Scrolls in 1955. At that time he stated:

It has even been said that the discoveries will revolutionize New Testament scholarship. This may perhaps cause some alarm. There is no danger, however, that our understanding of the New Testament will be so revolutionized by the Dead Sea Scrolls as to require a revision of any basic article of Christian faith. All scholars who have worked on the texts will agree that this has not happened and will not happen.[12]

Another book on the Dead Sea Scrolls came from Burrows in 1958 and went into its fourth printing in 1969. In it Burrows enunciated his earlier conclusion:

> What I meant by basic articles of faith was not those beliefs that mean most to me but the outstanding traditional tenets of the Christian churches through all the centuries. It is quite true that as a liberal Protestant I do not share all the beliefs of my more conservative brethren. It is my considered conclusion, however, that if one will go through any of the historic statements of Christian faith he will find nothing that has been or can be disproved by the Dead Sea Scrolls. This is as true of things that I myself do not believe as it is of my most firm and cherished convictions.[13]

THE RESURRECTION OF CHRIST

A very specific objection to Christianity involves attempting to trace the origin of the Resurrection narratives to pagan religions. The concept has taken various forms, and it was suggested again in Schonfield's book *The Passover Plot*. Specific and detailed response has been made to this book.[14] A persistent theory has been used to explain the idea of a bodily resurrection as an attempt to gain validation for a religion. The theory is this: There are several legendary accounts in the religions of the time of the rise of Christianity or thereabouts concerning the dying and rising again of the deity figures in these religions. This being true, it can be assumed, according to the theory, that Christian theological thinking about Jesus' resurrection had some ideological link with these world religions. Christian historian Edwin M. Yamauchi explains the background to this theory:

> The theory that there was a widespread worship of a dying-and-rising fertility god Tammaz in Mesopotamia, Adonis in Syria [note: not Galilee!], Attis in Asia Minor, and Osiris in Egypt—was propounded by Sir James Frazer in 1906. Schonfield rests his case on Theophile

Meek's interpretation of the Song of Solomon as a liturgy of an Adonis-Tammuz cult, which is in turn dependent upon Frazer's hypothesis.

The theory has been widely adopted by scholars who little realize its fragile foundations.[15]

Thus Schonfield implies that the ideological framework for the concept of the bodily resurrection of the Messiah came from these other world religions. He explicitly states that Jesus had some connection in His thinking with this concept and that this could form the basis for His plot to make people think He had actually died and was raised from the dead. Referring to Jesus as a "Nazorean," Schonfield stated:

> Thus we can appreciate how among the Saints belief in the Messiah could envisage both a Suffering Just One and a Glorious King. The two apparently distinct concepts could be united, the one preceding the other, as evidently they were in the mind of Jesus. It took a Nazarean of Galilee to apprehend from the Scriptures that death and resurrection was the bridge between the two phases. The very tradition of the land where Adonis yearly died and rose again seemed to call for it.[16]

It is pertinent for our discussion to outline Schonfield's position briefly before proceeding to answer this attempt to link Christ's resurrection with the legendary accounts in pagan religions of a dying and rising deity.

The real story behind the Christian message of a risen Savior is believed by Schonfield to be this: Jesus, determined to represent Himself as risen from the dead, devised a plot that would be executed with the help of Joseph of Arimathea and an unknown "young man." According to this plot, He was to be crucified, and He was to have arranged a fake death by being given a drug. Then His confidants were to take Him from the cross, and He would later appear, representing Himself as having arisen from the dead. The unexpected and unplanned action of the Roman soldier thrusting the spear into the side of Jesus really altered the original plot, according to Schonfield. His coconspirators quickly removed Him from the cross. Jesus regained consciousness for a short time, but died within hours. After the burial His body was removed from the tomb. One of His helpers, the "unknown young man," was repeatedly mistaken to actually be the risen Jesus by some of those early eyewitnesses, who thought they had seen Jesus. Many unsuspecting readers of Schonfield's book will conclude that this is really a true account that explains the idea of the bodily resurrection of Jesus. Schonfield himself states:

> We are nowhere claiming for our reconstruction that it represents what actually happened, but that on the evidence we have it may be fairly close to the truth. We have to allow that the Gospel accounts come to us from a time when the figure of Jesus had become larger than life, and his story had acquired in telling and retelling many legendary features. Yet we must not treat them as wholly fictitious and they have preserved valuable indications of what transpired. We can almost see the process at work which transformed the deep despondency of the companions of Jesus into the joyful conviction that he had triumphed over death as he said he would. What emerges from the records is that various disciples did see somebody, *a real living person*. Their experiences were not subjective.[17]

The total impression left in the book, as well as in the promotional advertisement on the back cover of the paperback edition, is that true scholarship has finally told the truth about the resurrection of Jesus.

The Response to This Position

It is not valid to assume a link between the resurrection of Jesus and the death and resurrection of pagan deity figures. John Gresham Machen (1881–1937) presented a painstaking historical refutation of this theory in his work entitled *The Origin of Paul's Religion* (first edition, 1925). One major problem for the theory is that most of the sources used in it come centuries after the time when they were supposed to have been influential in shaping the biblical account. Machen demonstrated this conclusively by citing the actual date of a quotation from Firmicus Maternus. According to advocates of the false theory, this quotation supposedly provided a clear link between the resurrection of a deity-figure in the oriental religion and the bodily resurrection of Christ. The assumption was made in the false theory that Paul was the key constructor of the theology of the resurrection of Jesus and that he was influenced by certain words in the quotation, or at least by some of its ideas. Machen cogently noted:

But the trouble is that Firmicus Maternus lived in the fourth century after Christ, three hundred years later than Paul. With what right can an utterance of his be used in the reconstruction of pre-Christian paganism? What would be thought, by the same scholars who quote Firmicus Maternus so confidently as a witness to first-century paganism, of a historian who should quote a fourth-century Christian writer as a witness to first-century Christianity?[18]

Machen then proceeded to respond to counterobjections in laying this false theory to rest.

Exemplifying the same kind of thorough research that Machen did, Edwin M. Yamauchi wrote a more recent work that can be cited in response to the attempt to establish a link between Jesus' resurrection and the stories of the rising from death of pagan deities. Yamauchi essentially approaches the evidence with a two-pronged counterattack. He shows, in the first place, the falsehood of what formerly had been assumed to be a bona fide account of a legendary resurrection of a deity figure in one of these religions. Certainly if it can be shown that the legend of a dying and rising deity has no basis, then any idea that the Christian interpretation of Jesus' death and resurrection was shaped by that legend, or influenced by it, is also false and irrelevant. No wonder Yamauchi said that this kind of theorizing has a fragile basis! He stated the evidence as follows:

> In recent years Samuel N. Kramer has made a thorough study of the Mesopotamian sources for the alleged resurrection of Tammuz by Ishtar, and has found that this popular belief was based on "nothing but inference and surmise, guess and conjecture." (*Mythologies of the Ancient World* [Garden City, N.Y.: Doubleday Anchor, 1961], p. 10.) In 1960 Kramer discovered a new poem, "The Death of Dumuzi (the Sumerian name for Tammuz)," which proves conclusively that instead of rescuing Tammuz from the underworld Ishtar sent him there as her substitute. (See the present writer's article, "Tammuz and the Bible," *Journal of Biblical Literature,* LXXXIV [1965], 283–90.) A line in a fragmentary and obscure text is the only positive evidence to indicate that after being sent to the underworld Tammuz himself may have had his sister take his place for half the year. (Cf. S. N. Kramer's note, *Bulletin of the American Schools of Oriental Research,* no. 183 [October, 1966]; 31.)[19]

In this kind of research Yamauchi virtually destroys the foundation of the false theory. He concluded that the other alleged resurrections of such deity figures as Adonis and Attis do not appear in the literature until long after the time when they were supposed to have been influential in shaping the Christian interpretation of Jesus' death and resurrection.

In the second instance, as another phase of his counterattack against this kind of theorizing, Yamauchi deals with the actual meaning of resurrection itself. He states:

> The death and resurrection of these various mythological figures, however attested, would in all cases typify the annual death and rebirth of vegetation. This significance cannot be attributed to the death and resurrection of Jesus. A. D. Nock sets forth the most striking contrast between pagan and Christian examples of resurrection as follows: "In Christianity everything is made to turn on a dated experience on a historical Person; it can be seen from I Cor. vx:3 [sic] that the statement of the story early assumed the form of a statement in a Creed. There is nothing in the parallel cases which points to any attempt to give such a basis of historical evidence to belief." (*Early Gentile Christianity and Its Hellenistic Background* [New York: Harper Torchbooks, 1964]; p. 107; cf. also Bruce Metzger, "Considerations of Methodology in the Study of the Mystery Religions and Early Christianity," *Harvard Theological Review*, XLVIII [1955], 1–20.)[20]

We have considered enough of the kind of work that Christian scholars have done to give a careful refutation of the attempts to link the Resurrection narratives with pagan sources. Again, it is a case of simply examining evidence, sifting sources, and letting the facts speak for themselves.

CONCLUSION

Concise consideration has been given to three questions in Christological apologetics. The purpose has been to state clearly a Christian response to what could be termed frontal assaults against the massive truth of Christ's entrance into time-space history, His life on this earth, and His death and resurrection. The need for stating the facts on which the Christian faith rests is ever present for each generation of believers. Peter provides a fitting summary for these selected areas in the history of Jesus Christ's birth, life, death, and resurrection: "For we did not follow cleverly devised tales when we made known to you the power and coming of our Lord Jesus Christ, but we were eyewitnesses of His majesty" (2 Peter 1:16).

REVIEW QUESTIONS

1. State concisely the major contrasts between pagan accounts of unusual births and the biblical account of the virgin birth of Christ.

2. Explain briefly the logical fallacy involved in assuming that since the pagan accounts of these unusual births were written before the Gospels, the writers of the Gospels used them for their background to the Virgin Birth account of Christ's entrance into the world.

3. What implications for Christianity are there in the kind of reasoning that would assume that Jesus spent time at Qumran and was influenced by the ideas taught there?

4. What does history state about Jesus' contact with the people at Qumran?

5. How can one argue against links between Jesus' teaching and the teachings from the books revealing the way of life followed at Qumran?

6. How does Matthew 15:11 speak against a teaching apparently held by Qumran adherents with reference to ceremonial baths and washings?

7. Besides legalism and washings, point out a couple of other areas where there is a contrast between the teaching of the Qumran sectarians and the teaching of Jesus.

8. What is the conclusion of Millar Burrows concerning the Dead Sea Scrolls and the basic articles of faith that constitute the historic doctrines of the Christian faith?

9. Explain very briefly the false theory linking legendary accounts of dying and rising deities with Jesus' resurrection.

10. Outline briefly Schonfield's theory about the Passover plot.

11. What major problem did Machen cite in connection with the false theory about the death and resurrection of deities?

12. Summarize in your own words Edwin Yamauchi's two-pronged counterattack against this theory.

FOR FURTHER READING

Gromacki, Robert Glenn. *The Virgin Birth: Doctrine of Deity*. Nashville: Thomas Nelson, 1974. Chaps. 18–20.

Machen, J. Gresham. *The Origin of Paul's Religion*. 1956. Reprint. Grand Rapids: Eerdmans, 1973.

Pfeiffer, Charles F. *The Dead Sea Scrolls and the Bible*. Grand Rapids: Baker, 1969. Chap. 9.

Yamauchi, Edwin M. "Appendix A: Passover Plot or Easter Triumph? A Critical Review of H. Schonfield's Recent Theory." In *Christianity for the Tough Minded*. Edited by John Warwick Montgomery. Minneapolis: Bethany, 1973.

CHAPTER 12

Conclusion

In this book I have identified and discussed some topics within the broad field of Christian apologetics. I have given suggested patterns for speaking the truth back into any non-Christian framework of thought. The level of challenge in the modern era for Christian defense is high, and there is much more work to do. The challenges come from a multiplicity of voices and positions seeking to reject the truth of Christianity and to establish a nontheistic and self-centered type of thinking and living. In radical contrast to these voices, historic biblical Christianity stands firmly on the Word of God as the position that alone is truth.

But I must sound a word of caution as we continue the task of applying various apologetic methods to the modern situation. Regardless of how we view apologetics, we cannot give it a place out of proportion to its intended role in the biblical perspective. The Scriptures very clearly give primary emphasis to the Great Commission and to the pattern of presenting the claims of Christ to a desperately needy world. In this light the role of apologetics is circumscribed and yet definite. It is not through argumentation alone that the work of the gospel is fostered but through the activity of our gracious God; so we need a balance here. We need to realize as apologetes that after all the arguments have been stated, at best we have invited those who bring reasoned objections against the faith to examine evidence, to think, to reflect, and to study the implications of their own position. But there will be no life-changing response to the gospel until there is obedience to the faith from the heart. Certainly, this truth moves us directly into the amazing realm of God's sovereign action and man's obedient response. We can hold the biblical tension here by believing firmly in both God's sovereignty and man's responsibility and by letting these two truths rest in perfect balance in biblical dimension.

Seen within this perfect balance of God's sovereign action and man's deep responsibility, the defense of the faith can move forward in obedience to the vital challenge stated in Scripture with the words that we studied earlier: "I felt the necessity to write to you appealing that you contend earnestly for the faith which was once for all delivered to the saints" (Jude 3).

Notes

Chapter 1

[1]Paul E. Holdcraft, ed., *Snappy Squibs for the Church Calendar* (Nashville: Abingdon, 1931), p. 106.

[2]William F. Arndt and F. Wilbur Gingrich, trans. and ed., *A Greek-English Lexicon of the New Testament and Other Early Christian Literature*, 4th rev. ed. (Chicago: University of Chicago Press, 1957), p. 95.

[3]Alan M. Stibbs, *The First Epistle General of Peter*, Tyndale New Testament Commentaries (Grand Rapids: Eerdmans, 1959), pp. 135–36.

[4]Arndt and Gingrich, *Greek-English Lexicon*, p. 95.

[5]Archibald Thomas Robertson, *Word Pictures in the New Testament*, 6 vols. (New York: Harper & Brothers, 1930), 3:416.

[6]W. H. Griffith Thomas, *Outline Studies in the Acts of the Apostles*, ed. Winifred T. Gillespie (Grand Rapids: Eerdmans, 1956), p. 445.

[7]George L. Lawlor, *The Epistle of Jude* (Nutley, N.J.: Presbyterian and Reformed, 1972), pp. 131–32.

[8]Cornelius Van Til, *Apologetics* (Nutley, N.J.: Presbyterian and Reformed, 1966), p. 2.

Chapter 2

[1]Cornelius Van Til, "Response by C. Van Til," in *Jerusalem and Athens*, ed. E. R. Geehan (Nutley, N.J.: Presbyterian and Reformed, 1971), p. 452.

[2]William F. Arndt and F. Wilbur Gingrich, trans. and ed., *A Greek-English Lexicon of the New Testament and Other Early Christian Literature*, 4th rev. ed. (Chicago: University of Chicago Press, 1957), p. 317.

[3]George W. Peters, *A Biblical Theology of Missions* (Chicago: Moody, 1972), p. 11.

[4]James I. Packer, *Evangelism and the Sovereignty of God* (Downers Grove, Ill.: InterVarsity, 1961), p. 41.

[5]Francis R. Beattie, *Apologetics*, vol. 1: *Fundamental Apologetics* (Richmond, Va.: The Presbyterian Committee of Publication, 1903), p. 42.

[6]Adapted and revised from a chart by Frederic R. Howe, in "Kerygma and Apologia," a chapter in *Jerusalem and Athens*, ed. Robert Geehan (Nutley, N.J.: Presbyterian and Reformed, 1971), p. 449.

[7]Viggo B. Olsen, *Daktar, Diplomat in Bangladesh* (Old Tappan, N.J.: Revell, Spire, 1975), p. 56.

Chapter 3

[1]F. F. Bruce, *Commentary on the Book of the Acts*, New International Commentary on the New Testament (Grand Rapids: Eerdmans, 1954), p. 133.

[2]Archibald Thomas Robertson, *Word Pictures in the New Testament*, 6 vols. (New York: Harper & Brothers, 1930), 3:76.

[3]Bruce, *Acts*, p. 141.

[4]F. F. Bruce, *The Defense of the Gospel in the New Testament*, rev. ed., (Grand Rapids: Eerdmans, 1977), pp. 18–19.

[5]Ibid., p. 20.

[6]Ibid., p. 40.

[7]Ned B. Stonehouse, *The Areopagus Address* (London: Tyndale, 1949), p. 25.

[8]Robertson, *Word Pictures in the New Testament*, 3:291.

[9]Bruce, *Acts*, pp. 363–64.

[10]W. Graham Scroggie, *Daily Notes* (London: Scripture Union, Sept.—Oct., 1955), n.p.

[11]Stonehouse, *Areopagus Address*, p. 37.

Chapter 4

[1]F. F. Bruce, *Paul, Apostle of the Heart Set Free* (Grand Rapids: Eerdmans, 1977), p. 408.

[2]Merrill C. Tenney, *New Testament Survey* (Grand Rapids: Eerdmans, 1961), p. 321.

[3]F. F. Bruce, *The Defense of the Gospel in the New Testament*, rev. ed. (Grand Rapids: Eerdmans, 1977), p. 78.

Chapter 5

[1]William Morris, ed., *The American Heritage Dictionary of the English Language* (New York: Houghton Mifflin, 1969), p. 1378.

[2]Ibid., p. 1086.

[3]Etienne Gilson, *History of Christian Philosophy in the Middle Ages* (New York: Random, 1955), p. 351.

[4]Martin Gardner, *Logic Machines and Diagrams* (New York: McGraw-Hill, 1958), p. 4.

[5]Bernard Ramm, *Problems in Christian Apologetics* (Portland, Ore.: Western Baptist Theological Seminary, 1949), p. 14.

[6]Sören Kierkegaard, *Concluding Unscientific Postscript*, trans. David F. Swenson (Princeton, N.J.: Princeton University Press, 1941), p. 504.

[7]A. H. Strong, *Systematic Theology* (Philadelphia: Judson, 1907), p. 839.

[8]Edward J. Carnell, *A Philosophy of the Christian Religion* (Grand Rapids: Eerdmans, 1952), pp. 478-79.

[9]Francis A. Schaeffer, *He Is There and He Is Not Silent* (Wheaton: Tyndale, 1972), p. 99.

[10]Ibid., p. 100.

[11]Benjamin B. Warfield, "Introductory Note," in Francis R. Beattie, *Apologetics, vol. 1: Fundamental Apologetics* (Richmond, Va.: Presbyterian Committee of Publication, 1903), p. 27.

[12]Ibid., pp. 24-25.

Chapter 6

[1]Norman L. Geisler, "'Avoid . . . Contradictions' (1 Timothy 6:20): A reply to John Dahms," *Journal of the Evangelical Theological Society*, vol. 22, no. 1 (March 1979): 64.

[2]Leon Morris, *The First Epistle of Paul to the Corinthians*, Tyndale New Testament Commentaries (Grand Rapids: Eerdmans, 1958), p. 42.

[3]Donald W. Burdick, "*Oida* and *ginōskō* in the Pauline Epistles," in *New Dimensions in New Testament Study*, Richard Longenecker and Merrill C. Tenney (Grand Rapids: Zondervan, 1974), pp. 344-56.

[4]Archibald Robertson and Alfred Plummer, *A Critical and Exegetical Commentary on the First Epistle of St. Paul to the Corinthians*, 2nd ed., The International Critical Commentary (Edinburgh: T. & T. Clark, 1914), p. 49.

[5]R. V. G. Tasker, *The Second Epistle of Paul to the Corinthians*, Tyndale New Testament Commentaries (Grand Rapids: Eerdmans, 1958), p. 70.

[6]Curtis Vaughan, *Ephesians: Bible Study Commentary* (Grand Rapids: Zondervan, 1977), pp. 99-100.

[7]Ibid., p. 100.

Chapter 7

[1]Norman L. Geisler, *Christian Apologetics* (Grand Rapids: Baker, 1976), p. 215.

[2]Vergilius Ferm, "Varieties of Naturalism," in *A History of Philosophical Systems*, ed. Vergilius Ferm (New York: Philosophical Library, 1950), p. 429.

[3]B. A. G. Fuller, "Naturalism," in *Dictionary of Philosophy*, Dagobert D. Runes (Totowa, N. J.: Littlefield, Adams, 1962), p. 205.

[4]See, for example, S. Morris Eames, *Pragmatic Naturalism* (Carbondale, Ill.: Southern Illinois University Press, 1977).

[5]James W. Sire, *The Universe Next Door* (Downers Grove, Ill.: Inter-Varsity, 1976), p. 73.

[6]*Humanist Manifestos I and II* (Buffalo, N.Y.: Prometheus, 1973), p. 8.

[7]Ibid., p. 16.

[8]W. G. T. Shedd, *Dogmatic Theology*, 3 vols. (1888; reprint edition, Grand Rapids: Zondervan, 1971), 1:210.

[9]Henry Clarence Thiessen, *Lectures in Systematic Theology*, rev. Vernon D. Doerksen (Grand Rapids: Eerdmans, 1979), p. 27.

[10]John Peter Lange, ed., *Commentary on the Holy Scriptures*, 25 vols. (1876; reprint edition, Grand Rapids: Zondervan, 1976), 20:82.

[11]John Murray, *The Epistle to the Romans*, 2 vols., New International Commentary on the New Testament (Grand Rapids: Eerdmans, 1968) 1:39–40.

[12]Ibid., 1:40.

[13]John H. Gerstner, "Reason and Revelation," in *Tenth: An Evangelical Quarterly*, vol. 9, no. 4 (October 1979): 2–3.

[14]Louis Berkhof, *Introductory Volume to Systematic Theology* (Grand Rapids: Eerdmans, 1932), p. 126.

[15]John C. Whitcomb, Jr., *The Origin of the Solar System* (Philadelphia: Presbyterian and Reformed, 1974), p. 30.

Chapter 8

[1]Hector Hawton, *Controversy* (Buffalo, N.Y.: Prometheus, 1971), pp. 24–25.

[2]Bertrand Russell, *Why I Am Not a Christian and Other Essays on Religion and Related Subjects*, ed. Paul Edwards (New York: Simon and Schuster, 1957), pp. 6–7.

[3]See, for example: Bruce R. Reichenbach, *The Cosmological Argument: A Reassessment* (Springfield, Ill.: Charles C. Thomas, 1972); Norman L. Geisler, *Philosophy of Religion* (Grand Rapids: Zondervan, 1974); William Lane Craig, *The Existence of God and the Beginning of the Universe* (San Bernardino, Calif.: Here's Life Publishers, 1979).

[4]See Henry M. Morris, "Thermodynamics and the Origin of Life," Institute for Creation Research (ICR) Impact Series no. 57, March 1978, for a careful response to the assumptions held by Prigogine on the second law of thermodynamics.

[5]Henry M. Morris, *The Scientific Case for Creation* (San Diego, Calif.: Creation-Life Publishers, 1977), pp. 14–16.

[6]Frederick Ferre, "Editor's Introduction," in *Natural Theology, Selections, William Paley* (New York: Bobbs-Merrill, 1963), pp. xxiii–xxiv.

[7]Robert Flint, *Theism* (New York: Scribner, 1905), p. 123.

[8]R. C. Sproul, *Objections Answered* (Glendale, Calif.: G/L Publications, 1978), p. 107.

[9]John H. Gerstner, *Reasons for Faith* (Grand Rapids: Baker, 1967), pp. 30–31.

[10]Norman L. Geisler, *Philosophy of Religion* (Grand Rapids: Zondervan, 1974), pp. 202–3.

[11]Ibid., p. 203.

[12]James O. Buswell, Jr., *A Systematic Theology of the Christian Religion*, 2 vols. in 1 vol. (Grand Rapids: Zondervan, 1962), p. 88.

[13]Hawton, *Controversy*, pp. 35–36.

[14]William Morris, ed., *The American Heritage Dictionary of the English Language* (New York: Houghton Mifflin, 1969), p. 866.

[15]Hawton, *Controversy*, p. 35.

[16]Charles F. Baker, *A Dispensational Theology* (Grand Rapids: Grace Bible College Publications, 1972), p. 119.

[17]Hawton, *Controversy*, p. 53.

[18]Geisler, *Philosophy of Religion*, p. 124.

[19]Russell, *Why I Am Not a Christian*, p. 12.

[20]Francis A. Schaeffer, *Genesis in Space and Time* (Downers Grove, Ill.: InterVarsity, 1972), p. 72.

[21]William Lane Craig, *The Existence of God and the Beginning of the Universe* (San Bernardino, Calif.: Here's Life Publishers, 1979), p. 10.

[22]Philip Edgcumbe Hughes, *A Commentary on the Epistle to the Hebrews* (Grand Rapids: Eerdmans, 1977), p. 462.

Chapter 9

[1]Bertrand Russell, *Why I Am Not a Christian and Other Essays on Religion and Related Subjects*, ed. Paul Edwards (New York: Simon and Schuster, 1957), p. 12.

[2]See, for example, R. Hooykaas, *Religion and the Rise of Modern Science* (Grand Rapids: Eerdmans, 1972).

[3]See, for example, Frank Morison, *Who Moved the Stone?* (London:

Faber and Faber, 1962); Josh McDowell, *Evidence That Demands a Verdict*, rev. ed. (San Bernardino, Calif: Here's Life Publishers, 1979), pp. 179–263.

[4]William Morris, ed., *The American Heritage Dictionary of the English Language* (New York: Houghton Mifflin, 1969), p. 455.

[5]Ibid., p. 1330.

[6]Ibid., p. 1047.

[7]Ibid., p. 279.

[8]John Calvin, *Institutes of the Christian Religion*, trans. Ford Lewis Battles, 2 vols., Library of Christian Classics (Philadelphia: Westminster Press, 1960), 1:92.

[9]Ibid., 1:79–80.

Chapter 10

[1]New York: Bantam, 1971.

[2]Jacques Barzun and Henry F. Graff, *The Modern Researcher*, rev. ed. (New York: Harcourt, Brace & World, 1970), p. 155.

[3]Louis Gottschalk, *Understanding History* (New York: Knopf, 1960), p. 150.

[4]Ibid.

[5]E. M. Blaiklock, *Layman's Answer* (London: Hodder and Stoughton, 1968), pp. 71–72.

[6]See, for example, Josh McDowell, *Evidence That Demands a Verdict*, rev. ed. (San Bernardino, Calif.: Here's Life Publishers, 1979), pp. 179–263.

[7]See F. F. Bruce, *The New Testament Documents: Are They Reliable?* 5th rev. ed. (Grand Rapids: Eerdmans, 1978).

[8]McDowell, *Evidence*, pp. 81–87.

[9]Josephus, *Antiquities*, trans. W. Whiston (Philadelphia: Winston, n.d.) 18.3.535.

[10]Gottschalk, *Understanding History*, p. 161.

[11]R. C. Stone; "Josephus," in *The Zondervan Pictorial Encyclopedia of the Bible*, 5 vols. (Grand Rapids: Zondervan, 1975) 3:697.

Chapter 11

[1]Hugh J. Schonfield, *The Passover Plot* (New York: Bantam, 1971), pp. 42–43.

[2]Ibid., p. 67.

[3]Robert Glenn Gromacki, *The Virgin Birth: Doctrine of Deity* (Nashville: Thomas Nelson, 1974), pp. 180–81.

[4]Thomas Boslooper, *The Virgin Birth* (Philadelphia: Westminster, 1962), p. 135.

[5]Gromacki, *Virgin Birth,* p. 180.

[6]Ibid., p. 179.

[7]Charles Francis Potter, *The Lost Years of Jesus Revealed,* 2nd ed. (New York: Crest, Fawcett Library, 1962), p. 100.

[8]Ibid., p. 123.

[9]Theodor H. Gastner, *The Dead Sea Scriptures,* rev. ed. (Garden City, N.Y.: Doubleday, Anchor, 1956), pp. 88–89.

[10]Charles F. Pfeiffer, *The Dead Sea Scrolls and the Bible* (Grand Rapids: Baker, 1969), p. 99.

[11]Potter, *Lost Years,* pp. 139–40.

[12]Millar Burrows, *The Dead Sea Scrolls* (New York: Viking, 1955), p. 327.

[13]Millar Burrows, *More Light on the Dead Sea Scrolls* (New York: Viking, 1958), p. 39.

[14]See, for example, Clifford Wilson *The Passover Plot Exposed* (San Diego, Calif.: Creation-Life Publishers, 1977).

[15]Edwin M. Yamauchi, "Appendix A: Passover Plot or Easter Triumph? A Critical Review of H. Schonfield's Recent Theory," in *Christianity for the Tough Minded,* ed. John Warwick Montgomery (Minneapolis, Minn.: Bethany, 1973), p. 263.

[16]Schonfield, *Passover Plot,* p. 219.

[17]Ibid., pp. 165–66.

[18]J. Gresham Machen, *The Origin of Paul's Religion,* (1965; reprint ed. Grand Rapids: Eerdmans, 1973), p. 237.

[19]Yamauchi, "Appendix A," p. 263.

[20]Ibid., pp. 263–64.

Selective Annotated Bibliography

A general and selective introductory bibliography for the field of Christian apologetics.

Blaiklock, E. M. *Layman's Answer*. London: Hodder and Stoughton, 1968. A trained classicist and historian responds to critical attacks against the historicity of the Christian faith.

Blaiklock, E. M., ed. *Why I Am Still a Christian*. Grand Rapids: Zondervan, 1971. A collection of twelve essays by internationally known Christian scholars. It gives ample evidence of the truthfulness of Christianity and its response to non-Christian positions. Such fields as philosophy, medicine, history, geography, and physics are concisely involved, representing the vocation of each of the authors.

Bruce, F. F. *The Defense of the Gospel in the New Testament*. Rev. ed. Grand Rapids: Eerdmans, 1977. A concise study of the early biblical defense of the faith made with reference to Judaism, paganism, the Roman Empire, and early forms of Gnosticism. It is valuable for its stress on a method of apologetics that is biblical.

Bruce, F. F. *The New Testament Documents: Are They Reliable?* 5th rev. ed. Grand Rapids: Eerdmans, 1960. A careful presentation of the case for the historical reliability of the source documents of Christianity.

Buell, Jon A., and Hyder, O. Quentin. *Jesus: God, Ghost or Guru?* Grand Rapids: Zondervan, 1980. This excellent work is part of the series in the Christian Free University Curriculum—books designed to state the Christian position in response to various secular fields or challenges from various world views opposed to Christianity. This book gives a critical analysis of attitudes toward Jesus that challenge His integrity, and it provides fitting responses to such attacks as that by Hugh Schonfield, for example.

Carnell, Edward J. *An Introduction to Christian Apologetics*. Grand Rapids: Eerdmans, 1950. A basic statement of the defense of biblical orthodoxy.

The author deals with specific problems, appeals to systematic consistency as a guide for building a defense, and handles such problems as evil, miracles, and faith and reason.

——. *A Philosophy of the Christian Religion*. Grand Rapids: Eerdmans, 1952. A major defense of Christian theism against selected leading schools of philosophy such as humanism and communism.

Chapman, Colin. *Christianity on Trial*. Wheaton, Ill.: Tyndale, 1975. This major work was originally published as three separate books in England. The author surveys basic world views and uses a question-and-answer method to deal with almost every major problem area facing Christianity. An excellent work.

Clark, Gordon H. *A Christian View of Men and Things*. Grand Rapids: Eerdmans, 1952. A Calvinist philosopher presents some of the issues pertinent to apologetics, such as how we can know God, good and evil, and Christian truth.

——. *Historiography, Secular and Religious*. Nutley, N.J.: Craig, 1971. A detailed study of historiography (the principles or methodology of historical study) from the Calvinist position. Vital questions are involved here for apologetics.

Close, Henry. *Reasons for Our Faith*. Richmond, Va.: John Knox, 1962. A brief survey of many different ways of defending the faith. Each chapter includes short questions for review and discussion, selected readings, and lists of further areas for research in other books. The author selects these methods on the basis of various starting points for defense, such as experience, God, man's needs, and nature.

Craig, William Lane. *The Existence of God and the Beginning of the Universe*. San Bernardino, Calif.: Here's Life Publishers, 1979. A Christian philosopher moves right into detailed and methodical argumentation for Christian theism. This is logical and coherent reasoning at its very best and is an excellent study.

Dulles, Avery. *A History of Apologetics*. Philadelphia: Westminster, 1971. A Catholic scholar provides a thorough study of the history of Protestant and Catholic apologetics up to the mid-twentieth century.

Geehan, E. R., ed. *Jerusalem and Athens. Critical Discussions on the Theology and Apologetics of Cornelius Van Til*. Nutley, N.J.: Presbyterian and Reformed, 1971. Articles contributed by many writers on varied themes of apologetics in honor of a veteran and distinguished Christian scholar, Cornelius Van Til. The work concerns itself with almost every problem in apologetics and with methods of defending the faith and it supplies the reader with Van Til's careful responses to many of the positions. An excellent study and useful as a tool.

Geisler, Norman L. *Christian Apologetics*. Grand Rapids: Baker, 1976. A major treatment of a total defense of Christian theism from a trained philosopher and apologete. The author surveys major systems of apologetics, deals definitively with most major nontheistic approaches, and builds a system of defense of the Christian position creatively and logically. An excellent tool in the evaluation of non-Christian positions.

_____. *Philosophy of Religion*. Grand Rapids: Zondervan, 1974. As is often the case, some of the areas of apologetics are dealt with in this work on the philosophy of religion. The author deals exhaustively with the arguments for the existence of God (offering the most comprehensive treatment of this subject known to this writer) and the problem of evil, along with other topics.

_____. *The Roots of Evil*. Grand Rapids: Zondervan, 1978. This work goes right to the heart of the problem of evil, sets forth biblical guidelines, and works through the issues. An excellent guide and tool.

Gerstner, John H. *Reasons for Faith*. Grand Rapids: Baker, 1967. A concise and closely reasoned approach to varied topics in apologetics. This work is virtually a complete handbook and treatment of all the questions in apologetics from a defensible and consistent position.

Habermas, Gary R. *The Resurrection of Jesus: An Apologetic*. Grand Rapids: Baker, 1980. A closely reasoned and thoroughly developed apologetic for all of Christian theism. The author carefully develops an integrated system of apologetics with the resurrection of Christ placed in the key position for the elements. The book is an excellent theological study, with a careful analysis of the role of the Holy Spirit in Christian apologetics.

Hackett, Stuart C. *The Resurrection of Theism*. Chicago: Moody, 1957. A defense of Christian theism based on an honest effort to balance reason and revelation. Hackett presents a rational system as a basis for theism and grounds his apologetic in the area of the categories of the mind, reflecting on his analysis of Kant. This is thought-provoking and stimulating.

Haentzschel, Ad. *How About Christianity?* St. Louis: Concordia, 1961. A short introduction to apologetics, organized around basic questions asked by those who are testing and seeking information about Christianity. He deals briefly with some objections.

Hamilton, Floyd. *The Basis of Christian Faith*. New York: Harper & Row, 1964. The latest revision of a major work on apologetics from the rich tradition of the so-called "Old Princeton" school of apologetics. This work deals with just about every phase of Christian apologetics, from various philosophies to arguments against the Bible and selected critical problems.

Keyser, Leander S. *A System of Christian Evidence*. 10th rev. ed. Burlington, Iowa: Lutheran Literary Board, 1953. A helpful combination of philosophical apologetics and Christian evidences. Many objections are dealt with, and bibliographies are supplied at the end of the work. Some of the material is out of date, but there is enough help here to warrant serious study.

Lewis, Gordon R. *Judge for Yourself: A Workbook on Contemporary Challenges to Christian Faith*. Downers Grove, Ill: InterVarsity, 1974. A very practical and helpful study of some major problem areas in apologetics. The areas include the exclusiveness of Christianity as the only way to God, the problem of evil, miracles, and the question of those who have never heard of Christianity. The approach follows a self-study method, involving the reader directly in the learning process.

_____. *Testing Christianity's Truth Claims: Approaches to Christian Apologetics*. Chicago: Moody, 1976. A major work that lucidly describes many systematic approaches to apologetics, majoring on the one followed by E. J. Carnell. This excellent work offers a careful analysis of major systems of defense and contains a wealth of material.

Lewis, C. S. *Mere Christianity*. New York: Macmillan, 1957. A defense of Christianity on the basis of the moral law as an integral part of the universe. Included in this work are clarifications of what Christians believe and a logical statement of Christian theism.

_____. *Miracles, A Preliminary Study*. New York: Macmillan, 1966. One of the very best overall studies of the defense of the faith with reference to those who question the miracles of Scripture.

Linton, Irwin H. *A Lawyer Examines the Bible*. 1943. Reprints. Grand Rapids: Baker, 1974. San Diego: Creation-Life, 1978. A member of the bar of the District of Columbia wrote this work, which presents a selective treatment of evidence for Christianity from the viewpoint of legal evidence and the securing of a verdict.

Little, Paul E. *Know Why You Believe*. Rev. ed. Downers Grove, Ill: InterVarsity, 1968. Practical and up-to-date responses to honest inquiries concerning Christian theism. Among the specific areas treated concisely are the resurrection of Christ, the existence of God, miracles, the problem of evil, and the unique claims of Christianity.

Machen, J. Gresham. *Christianity and Liberalism*. 1923. Reprint. Grand Rapids: Eerdmans, 1956. Not technically a treatment of apologetics, but vital to a general clarification of what historic orthodoxy is and to its defense against the older liberal theology. This is must reading for any Christian in the modern era, for its clear and readable format sets forth exactly what it is that Christians are seeking to defend in apologetics.

McDowell, Josh. *Evidence That Demands a Verdict.* rev. ed. San Bernardino, Calif: Here's Life Publishers, 1979. This is a masterpiece of thorough documentation. It is readable and highly useful to the Christian in presenting apologetics at the cutting edge of reality. It presents detailed work in evidences for the truth claims of Christianity, the Scriptures, the centrality of Christ, and His claims. It is a gold mine of valuable material and easily ranks as the finest work on Christian evidences available.

_____. *More Evidence that Demands a Verdict.* vol. 2. San Bernardino, Calif.: Here's Life Publishers, 1975. This sequel to the first volume deals primarily with the battleground of higher criticism and the Bible, since many of the questions relative to Christianity's truth claims rest in this area.

_____. *More Than a Carpenter.* Wheaton, Ill.: Tyndale, 1977. A short and readable presentation of evidences for the truthfulness of Christianity that is primarily Christological in nature. The author appeals to the validity of historical tests and evidence.

_____. *The Resurrection Factor.* San Bernardino, Calif.: Here's Life Publishers, 1981. An excellent and analytical study of the historical evidence for the resurrection of Jesus Christ. Well outlined and organized, this book puts together a wealth of material for the defender of the faith.

McDowell, Josh, and Stewart, Don. *Answers to Tough Questions.* San Bernardino, Calif: Here's Life Publishers, 1980. Concise but careful answers are given to many questions that skeptics ask about Christianity. The questions and answers deal with the Bible, Jesus Christ, God, miracles, Bible difficulties, world religions, Christian conversion, believing faith, the Shroud of Turin, and creation accounts.

Montgomery, John Warwick, ed. *Christianity for the Tough Minded.* Minneapolis: Bethany, 1973. A series of essays touching on many modern themes related to apologetics. The book is valuable for its unusual variety and its responses to claims such as those in Hugh J. Schonfield's *Passover Plot.*

Montgomery, John Warwick. *Faith Founded on Fact.* Nashville: Thomas Nelson, 1978. A thorough exposition of pertinent apologetic topics, including some essays that have appeared in other collections. The concepts presented here in such essays as "Can Faith Rest on Fact?" "The Place of Reason in Christian Witness," and "Science, Theology and the Miraculous" are well articulated and reasonable.

_____. *History and Christianity.* Downers Grove, Ill.: InterVarsity Press, 1972. An able Christian scholar and historian-philosopher presents the gist of the case for Christian theism as it touches on its historical foundation and roots.

———. *How Do We Know There Is a God?* Minneapolis: Bethany, 1973. A short treatment of many questions, giving very concise and cogent answers to questions pertinent to apologetics such as the nature of God, His existence, creation, and miracles.

———. *The Shape of the Past,* rev. ed. Minneapolis: Bethany, 1975. A careful groundwork is laid here in historiography for the historicity of Scripture and for a Christian philosophy of history that is objective rather than subjective.

———. *Where Is History Going?* Minneapolis: Bethany, 1972. A careful historiographical masterpiece, elucidating a definitive answer to relativism in historiography and setting forth the foundation of Christian truth solidly on historical groundwork. This is an excellent work.

Morison, Frank. *Who Moved the Stone?* 1930. Reprint. Grand Rapids: Zondervan, 1980. A classic study on the evidence for the resurrection of Christ. It has gone through many successive printings and two editions. It is thorough, analytical, and, in the best sense of the word, historical. This is a good background for the Christian response to Hugh J. Schonfield in his attack on Christianity found in his book *The Passover Plot* (1969).

Morris, Henry M. *Many Infallible Proofs.* San Diego, Calif.: Creation-Life Publisher, 1974. This book is a good presentation of Christian evidences, well-documented, carefully indexed, and thorough.

Morris, Thomas V. *Francis Schaeffer's Apologetics: A Critique.* Chicago: Moody, 1976. Valuable for its thought-provoking and analytical study of the apologetics of Schaeffer. The author possibly underestimates Schaeffer's methodology, particularly in the area of the work of the Holy Spirit in final verification of Christianity.

Nash, Ronald H., ed. *The Philosophy of Gordon H. Clark.* Nutley, N.J.: Presbyterian and Reformed, 1968. A series of scholarly articles honoring Gordon H. Clark (distinguished Calvinist philosopher) and presenting many areas of vital interest to the student of apologetics. The chief value of such essays in collections like this volume is in the contribution made for comparing various viewpoints in apologetics and in seeing how Clark responds personally to selected authors.

Orr, James. *The Christian View of God and the World.* Grand Rapids: Eerdmans, 1947. A reprint of a classic statement of Christian theism from a philosophical point of view.

Orr, J. Edwin. *The Faith That Persuades.* New York: Harper and Row, 1977. The author is a trained historian, holding an earned doctorate in philosophy from Oxford. He writes this highly enjoyable work (a new edition of his *Faith That Makes Sense*) on apologetics from a very practical vantage point. Much of it grew out of his discussions with inquirers and seekers that he conducted as a military chaplain and speaker at various campus meetings.

_____. *100 Questions About God.* Glendale, Calif.: Gospel Light, 1966. Highly interesting discussions about many of the problems within apologetics.

Packer, James I. *Fundamentalism and the Word of God.* Grand Rapids: Eerdmans, 1958. This work is not limited to apologetics, but includes chapters on faith and reason that are outstanding. Faith and reason are involved in apologetics, and Packer's treatment of them gives real balance and help to the defender of the faith.

Pinnock, Clark H. *Set Forth Your Case.* Chicago: Moody, 1973. A spokesman for a solid use of evidence and objectivity in defense, Pinnock sets the case for Christianity squarely on the ground of history and cogently shows the tragic weakness of humanism and other systems opposed to Christianity.

Ramm, Bernard. *A Christian Appeal to Reason.* Waco: Word, 1977. A recent study by a scholar who is a master apologete and works within a basically Calvinistic framework. He has done extensive work with students in helping to prepare them to reach other students for Christ in witness and defense. The work is essentially an attempt to state a coherent system of apologetics and deals with such topics as theistic proofs, the problem of evil, and faith and reason. It was originally published in 1972 as *The God Who Makes a Difference.*

_____. *The Pattern of Authority.* Grand Rapids: Eerdmans, 1957. This is a basic study of the ultimate authority of the Word of God and the work of the Holy Spirit in sealing the Word. It is listed here with works on apologetics because it deals with the crucial question of religious authority and because of its treatment of systems that oppose biblical orthodoxy.

_____. *Problems in Christian Apologetics.* Portland, Ore.: Western Baptist Seminary Press, 1949. This is the substance of four lectures delivered by the author at Western Conservative Baptist Seminary in 1948. The work deals with some really basic issues in apologetics and gives a good summary of four methods of defense.

_____. *Protestant Christian Evidences.* Chicago: Moody, 1953. A major work that covers most of the traditional avenues of presenting evidence for the truthfulness of biblical theism. The author deals with the question of fulfilled prophecy, miracles, and the resurrection of Christ. Cogent and careful answers are given to philosophical naturalism.

_____. *Varieties of Christian Apologetics.* Grand Rapids: Baker, 1961. A basic study of the philosophical questions involved in apologetics. It involves an analytical study of systems of apologetics and gives careful studies of Pascal, Butler, and Kuyper, among others. The work is an excellent guide to the correlation of theology, philosophy, and apologetics.

Reid, J. K. S. *Christian Apologetics*. Grand Rapids: Eerdmans, 1969. A well-written and analytical history of apologetics.

Ridenour, Fritz, ed. *Who Says?* Glendale, Calif.: Gospel Light Publications, 1967. Written for the high-school age level, this work is a discussion of many of the basic issues involved in apologetics and can easily be adapted to any age group.

Runia, Klaas. *I Believe in God*. Downers Grove, Ill.: InterVarsity, 1963. A short, concise appraisal of the theology of the orthodox creeds and an excellent critique of neoorthodoxy, neoliberalism, radical theology, and other deviations from orthodoxy. The work is valuable to the student of apologetics for its relationship to theology.

Schaeffer, Francis A. *Escape From Reason*. London: Inter-Varsity, 1968. A penetrating study of some of the issues that make up backgrounds to apologetics. It is written from the viewpoint of the late 1960s and addresses the philosophical attitude of despair that had permeated much of the intellectualism of that era. The author provides an intelligent defense of orthodox biblical Christianity in response to this mood.

_____. *The God Who Is There*. Downers Grove, Ill.: InterVarsity, 1968. The author has a sweeping knowledge of art, philosophy, history, literature, modern drama, film, and culture. Within a basically Calvinistic and modern presuppositionalist framework, he uncovers the core of the thinking processes of the unregenerate person and forces him or her to come face to face with inherent presuppositions and needs.

_____. *He Is There and He Is Not Silent*. Wheaton, Ill.: Tyndale, 1972. Schaeffer explains that one should read his works in the following order: first, *The God Who Is There*, then *Escape From Reason*, and finally this one. Schaeffer deals carefully with religious epistemology and knowledge bases for systems of reality. (I classify him as a modern or moderate presuppositionalist.)

Sire, James W. *The Universe Next Door: A Basic World View Catalog*. Downers Grove, Ill.: InterVarsity, 1976. A thorough review of many systems of thought, including deism, naturalism, nihilism, existentialism, Eastern pantheistic monism, and the new consciousness. This book offers excellent help in apologetics, for the author shows inconsistencies in the non-Christian positions and sets forth the view of theism as a workable and meaningful answer to all the others.

Smith, Wilbur M. *Therefore Stand*. 1945. Reprint. Grand Rapids: Baker, 1974. This is a classic in the sense that it includes detailed source material in the field of apologetics. Statements made by great thinkers and scientists when faced with the inevitability of death are given as an appeal to the apologetic value of Christian experience as a contrast to these conclusions of unbelief.

Sproul, R. C. *If There Is a God, Why Are There Atheists?* Minneapolis: Bethany, 1978. The author is a Calvinist scholar, staff theologian for Ligonier Valley Study Center, and a distinguished defender of total inerrancy. He gives here a detailed study of the psychology of atheism and makes a strong appeal for straight thinking based on the Scriptures. This is an excellent response to atheism.

_____. *Objections Answered.* Glendale, Calif: G/L Publications, 1978. This book contains some of the very best work in apologetics at the cutting edge of answering tough questions. Sproul deals with many of the great questions, such as the problem of evil, the existence of God, and criticism of the church. This material is really worth using in dialogues with non-Christian objectors who need help.

Van Til, Cornelius. *Apologetics. A Syllabus.* Nutley, N.J.: Presbyterian and Reformed, 1966. In this well-written and careful work, Van Til places before readers his position on the defense of the faith—a defense that is anchored to his basic theological vantage point and interpretation of Calvinism. This is must reading for all students of apologetics, regardless of what system they espouse.

_____. *The Defense of The Faith.* 3rd ed. Nutley, N.J.: Presbyterian and Reformed, 1967. This is a major treatment of the defense of the faith from the distinguished author's interpretation of Reformed theology. All defenders of the faith are indebted to Van Til for his careful workmanship and his absolute faithfulness to the inerrant Word of God. Van Til carries the position of Kuyper into its fullest implications as to the *place* and role of apologetics in the theological encyclopedia.

Williams, Rheinallt Nantlais. *Faith, Facts, History, Science, and How They Fit Together.* Wheaton, Ill.: Tyndale, 1974. An American printing of the work of a Christian philosopher in England. This is a fine treatment of the themes reiterated in the title, with an appeal to a faithful use of reason. Very well done.

Whitcomb, John C., Jr. *The Origin of the Solar System.* Philadelphia: Presbyterian and Reformed, 1974. A careful and well-documented study of the problems faced by non-Christian systems of thought in the matter of the origin of the universe. The work is vitally relevant for apologetics and reveals the staggering problems faced by nontheists. Also, the author gives a thorough and capable refutation of the so-called double-revelation theory, a theory that ultimately questions the full authority of Scripture.

Wilson, Clifford. *The Passover Plot Exposed.* San Diego, Calif.: Creation-Life Publishers, 1977. A careful and thorough response from a Christian scholar to the work by Schonfield.

General Index

Apologetics
  compared with evangelism, 30
  defined, 20
  and philosophy, 21–23
  related to an apology, 21
  and theology, 20
Areopagus, 41
Athens, 40

Berkhof, Louis, on relationship of
  natural and special revelation,
  85
Blaiklock, E. M., on the factuality of
  Christ's resurrection, 124–25
Boslooper, Thomas, on analyzing
  the pagan origin of Virgin
  Birth narratives, 135
Bruce, F. F.
  on the Colossian problem, 48, 51
  on the defense of Christ's
  crucifixion, 37–38
  on describing Mars Hill, 41–42
  on Stephen's defense, 34
Buswell, J. O., Jr., on the teleological argument, 94

Calvin, John, on evidence and defense, 114–15
Carnell, Edward J., on a critique of
  Kierkegaard, 58–59
Common ground, 65
Cosmological argument
  objections to, 89
  restudied and restated, 89–93
  stated, 88–89
Craig, W. L., on arguing for God's
  existence, 101

Democritus, 41

Epicureans, 40–41
Epicurius, 41
Evangelism
  contrasted with apologetics in
  data, 28–29
  contrasted with apologetics in
  demands placed on workers,
  29–30
  contrasted with apologetics in
  description, 26–28
  defined, 25–26
Evidence, defined, 111

Faith
  described, 53
  three constituent elements analyzed, 58
  true faith contrasted with the
  existentialist concept, 60
Ferre, Frederick, on objections to
  infinite regress, 90

Geisler, Norman L.
  on the cosmological argument,
  92–93
  on the validity of logical thinking, 66
Gerstner, John H.
  on the problem of causation,
  91–92
  on the relationship of revelation
  and reason, 84
Gottschalk, Louis, on the tests for
  verifying historical accuracy,
  123–24

Scripture Index